Places to Be

tra ...of
...vs

**Includes venues in France, Greece, India, Ireland, Italy, Portugal, Spain, Sri Lanka and Turkey.
Plus a selection of Alternative Holiday and Tour Operators!**

2004

Edited by Jonathan How and William Morris

Places to Be 2004
© Coherent Visions 2003
ISBN: 0 9524396 6 2

Editing and Design
Jonathan How and William Morris

Publisher
Coherent Visions
BCM Visions, London
WC1N 3XX
0870 444 2566
info@places-to-be.com

Printer
Lockholt & Co Ltd
1 St James's Street Mews
Brighton
BN2 1RT
01273 570077
lockholts@aol.com

Distributor
(trade and mail order)
Edge of Time Ltd
BCM Edge, London
WC1N 3XX
0800 083 0451
sales@edgeoftime.co.uk

Contents

- **4** Introduction
- **8** Getting Started

Main Listings

- **10** Venues in Scotland
- **22** Venues in the North of England
- **35** Venues in the East of England
- **40** Venues in the Midlands
- **47** Venues in Wales
- **65** Venues in South West England
- **96** Venues in South East England
- **111** Venues Outside the UK
- **133** Holiday and Tour Operators

Indexes

- **139** B&B Seeker's Index
- **142** Retreat Seeker's Index
- **146** Workshop Seeker's Index
- **152** Venue Seeker's Index
- **157** Alphabetical Index

Introduction

This book is the key to many wonderful places and experiences.

You can find congenial places to stay on a walking or cycling tour; you can discover a venue for that circle dance weekend you are planning. You can look up places that run retreats, and others that may have shamanic drumming workshops. There are places where you can find healing and recuperation or simply pamper yourself.

If you have the chance to go away for a weekend, a week, or more, why not try one of the many experiences on offer in this book? It is likely that not only will you return refreshed and revitalised, but that you will meet others who share your beliefs and way of life. Many of the places and holiday operators in this book are inspired by political and/or spiritual beliefs, and many are aware of the need to create a sustainable, Earth-friendly way of being. You have the chance to travel to beautiful and unusual places in the world and experience living in harmony with the landscape and culture. Look out for the eco-tourism features which many venues and organisations describe.

Several of the venues in this book are set in intentional communities of people living co-operatively. Age after age these places have been on the forward edge of social change, and if you are interested in this way of life, or of making links to it, then the events that they run provide a wonderful opportunity.

All of the venues and holidays in Places to Be are special in some way, offering something that you won't often find. In these pages we have tried to indicate which venues and holidays offer only vegetarian food, which have disabled access and which are particularly welcoming to lesbians and gay men.

Just as importantly, you can can use the indexes to find,

amongst other things, which places welcome children, and which have child-minding facilities. So you as parents can go to workshops, or just be on your own for a while.

If you are looking for a venue for a group you are organising, you will find that a lot of the relevant hiring information is now concentrated in one place on a venue's page.

As editors of this book, we allow venue and holiday operators to write at length about themselves, so you get a real flavour of how they are. Many also have websites, where you can read more, and often see helpful pictures.

Our own website, places-to-be.com, offers useful search facilities, and is updated during the year so you can be as sure as possible of having up-to-date information.

You will find that the book is divided into regions within the UK and countries outside the UK. In addition there is the popular section devoted to holiday and tour operators. As well as the full page entries which many venues desire, there are additional listings of other known venues. These are places whose existence we are fairly sure of (eg they have current websites) but for one reason or another they haven't replied to our requests for information.

Never just turn up at any of the places listed in this book. Always make arrangements beforehand and in this way you will be sure of a welcome. The essential prerequisite of a positive retreat experience.

We wish you fruitful searches and happy times!

If you enjoy this book then you may be interested in other products distributed by Edge of Time. Phone for a catalogue on 0800 083 0451 or visit **www.edgeoftime.co.uk**.

Diggers & Dreamers

This directory is known as the communard's bible and its new small format is proving very popular. It gives you an up-to-date directory of more than 80 existing and embryonic communities within the UK. Everything from Anarres to Zion!

The 2004/05 edition also features: a useful cross-index to help you find the community that matches your preferences; icons indicating how each community operates (on financial and sustainability levels); 10 myths of communal living exploded; a listing of Networks and Support Organisations

Utopia Britannica: British Utopian Experiments 1325 - 1945

Utopia Britannica is a tour-de-utopia: a journey through the hopes and dreams of our ancestors. Take a trip in the company of past generations of practical utopians: walk through the corridors of Harmony Hall with Robert Owen, stroll down the lanes of a Chartist land colony with the settlers from northern industrial towns, sing hymns of sacred sexuality with the Moravians or dream of Anarchy in the Cotswolds.

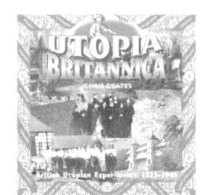

Moonwise Calendar

In this lunar calendar the months begin with New Moon, moon phases are shown for each night, and there are festivals and secular holidays from all round the world. All this plus fabulous illustrations. The Moonwise Calendar is of particular interest to Pagans, useful for people of many traditions, and full of information and inspiration. An unusual and fascinating gift for your friends, family and self!

Moonwise Diary

This companion to the Moonwise Calendar is easy to use, with four pages for each week. It contains daily astrological information and moon phases; clock times for Britain and Ireland; rising and setting of sun and moon for London, Glasgow and Dublin; as well as outstanding artwork and writing contributed by readers. Small enough to go in your bag or pocket, this diary allows you to work closely with the cycles of the moon, the planets and the peoples of the Earth.

Neal's Yard Agency

If you are seeking,
then you will find . . .
at
'The Travel Agent
for Inner Journeys'

**The UK's leading source of information
for Yoga, creativity & wellbeing holidays**

meditation, massage, creative writing, singing, dancing, simply 'being', unspoilt locations, yurts, tree houses, hammocks, like-minded company, laughter, fun, discovery ...

For free Holiday & Events Guide
contact
Neal's Yard Agency
BCM Neal's Yard • London WC1N 3XX • UK
Tel 0870 444 2702 • info@nealsyardagency.com
www.nealsyardagency.com

Getting started

The bulk of the book is made up of national and regional sections containing the detailed description of fixed venues. If you're just idly browsing then this is the place to do it!

The maps are also very useful overviews of what is available in Scotland, Wales and the English regions. **Look out especially for the places shown in bold, as these have full page entries.**

B&Bs

The B&Bs listed in **Places to Be** are all different in some way, even if that way is simply that they offer vegetarian food (however, this book does not claim to contain a comprehensive listing of vegetarian B&Bs to which several good guides exist already). Many of those in **Places to Be** are representative of a new breed of B&B which offer something more than just food and accommodation. Perhaps it is some kind of educational service, perhaps a healing therapy.

Retreats

People have been going on retreats for hundreds, if not thousands, of years. This ancient form of getting away from it all is rising in popularity again, notably amongst people who do not see themselves as attached to a particular religion. Many Christian establishments cater for this demand, often on a large scale. There are also a growing number of smaller venues offering retreats. You need to check whether the retreats are for individuals or groups; whether they are based on any particular spiritual system; how much guidance is available and/or how much you will be left to your own devices.

Retreat Seeker's Index
page 142

B&B Seeker's Index
page 139

Holiday and Tour Operators

The organisations listed on **pages 133-138** run either touring holidays or else events at a number of venues – some within and some outside the United Kingdom.

Workshops

If you're keen to participate in workshops and courses then head for the **Workshop Seeker's Index**. Here venues are shown with subject speciality headings. Of course, these categories can only be a very crude guide; a place offering walking, for example, will be included within the "Outdoor activities and sport" category. Often the text on the venue's page is more specific, but do look at their websites and/or contact them for more detailed information.

Workshop Seeker's Index page 146

Venues

If you run courses or workshops yourself then you'll be wanting the **Venue Seeker's Index**. You'll probably find it easiest to start with the approximate numbers of bedspaces. Where possible the index shows prices, a level of wheelchair access and a number of other accommodation features. You can usually find more specifics in the full pages entries. Always contact the venue for more details and to check that the information has not changed.

Venue Seeker's Index page 152

Map of Scotland: page 10

Details of subject specialities: page 146

Feature on our website: page 152

Full Page Entries

Venues are arranged alphabetically within nation and region. The text is written by the people who run the venues and tours, and give a good flavour of each. We have also asked them to bring out for you various areas such as **spiritual focus, eco-tourism features** and **public transport access.**

Many organisations list broad areas of **Subject specialities.** See the Workshop Seeker's Index for more on these. **Suitability and Specialism** indicates courses and holidays aimed at or premises suited to particular groups.

Getting started

Scotland

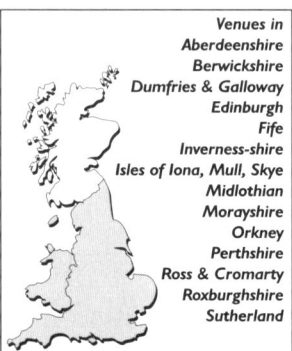

Venues in
Aberdeenshire
Berwickshire
Dumfries & Galloway
Edinburgh
Fife
Inverness-shire
Isles of Iona, Mull, Skye
Midlothian
Morayshire
Orkney
Perthshire
Ross & Cromarty
Roxburghshire
Sutherland

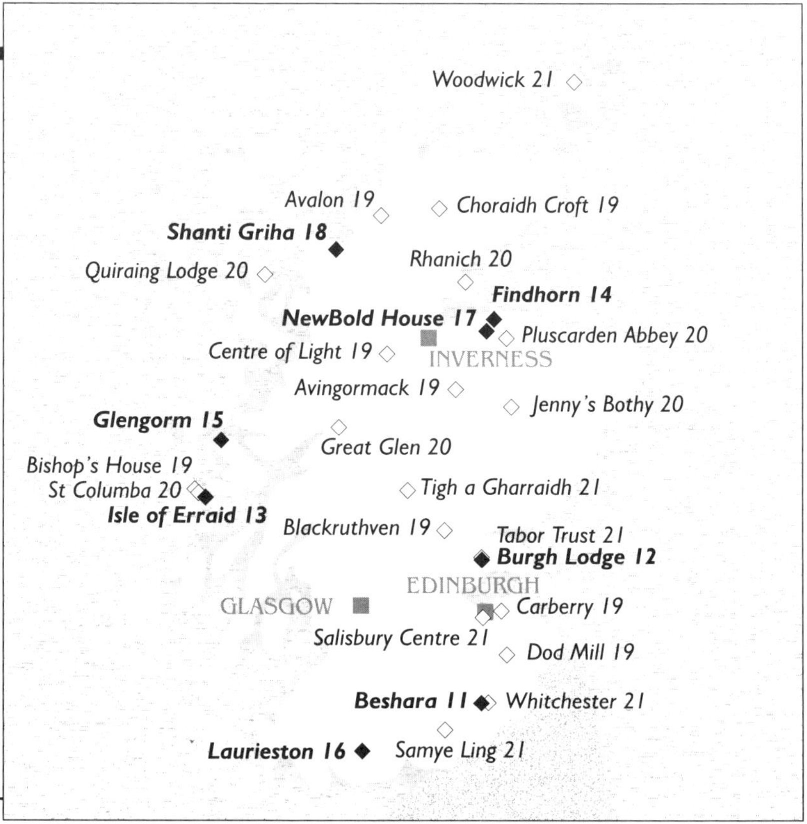

Woodwick 21 ◇

Avalon 19 ◇   ◇ Choraidh Croft 19
Shanti Griha 18 ◆
Quiraing Lodge 20 ◇   Rhanich 20 ◇
Findhorn 14 ◆
NewBold House 17 ◆
Centre of Light 19 ◇   ◇ Pluscarden Abbey 20
INVERNESS
Avingormack 19 ◇
Glengorm 15 ◆   ◇ Jenny's Bothy 20
Great Glen 20 ◇
Bishop's House 19 ◇
St Columba 20 ◇   ◇ Tigh a Gharraidh 21
Isle of Erraid 13 ◆
Blackruthven 19 ◇   Tabor Trust 21 ◇
Burgh Lodge 12 ◆
EDINBURGH
GLASGOW ■
Carberry 19 ◆
Salisbury Centre 21 ◇
◇ Dod Mill 19
Beshara 11 ◆ Whitchester 21 ◇
◇
Laurieston 16 ◆ Samye Ling 21 ◇

http://www.beshara.org

Beshara School

Courses of the Beshara School are concerned solely with the knowledge of the essential unity of all existence, by way of knowing one's own reality. This knowledge lies at the heart of all spiritual traditions and approaches to truth, and yet is not confined to any of them; consequently the Beshara School is open to students of any nationality or background, irrespective of creed. Courses are all-inclusive and fully residential, and comprise a balanced programme of study, work, meditation and spiritual practice. They range from a weekend to six months. Six-month courses, which have been running since 1975, begin on 1st October each year. Shorter courses run throughout the year, and visitors are welcome at any time. Chisholme House, the home of the school, is a Georgian country house and estate set in the vibrant beauty of the Scottish Borders.

Stuart Kenner
Chisholme House
Roberton
Hawick
Roxburghshire
TD9 7PH

✆ 01450 880215
✆ 01450 880204
✉ secretary@beshara.org

✔ Own Course Programme

🛏 30 bedspaces.
🚌 ... from South ... train/bus to Carlisle then Borders Rail Link Bus 195 to Hawick
... from North ... train/bus to Edinburgh then bus 95 to Hawick from St Andrews Sq Bus Terminal
Taxi or call for lift from Hawick

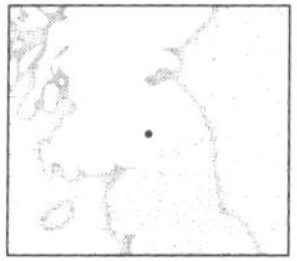

Scotland/Roxburghshire

The Burgh Lodge

🌐 http://www.burghlodge.co.uk

Camilla Storrie
The Burgh Lodge
Back Wynd, Falkland
Cupar, Fife
KY15 7BX
✆ 01337 857710
✆ 01337 858861
✉ burgh.lodge@btconnect.com

✓ **Bed & Breakfast**

⌁ 37 bedspaces (2 twins, 2 family rooms, 2 x 4-bedded rooms, one 8-bedded dormitory).

♿ Two rooms on the ground floor have specially adapted shower and toilet facilities.

🚉 Nearest railway station Ladybank 4 miles, or bus to Glenrothes and change to Bus 36 or 66, get off at Falkland - 2 minute walk to Lodge.

The Burgh Lodge offers 4 Star value-for-money hostel-style accommodation with a relaxed and friendly atmosphere where guests always receive the warmest of welcomes. Guests can enjoy reading in front of our log fire or explore the medieval and picturesque village of Falkland. A sense of tranquillity and timelessness remains throughout making it an ideal rural getaway for those tired of the City, yet it is within easy reach of Edinburgh, Perth, Stirling, Dundee and St Andrews.
The Lodge is surrounded by magnificent walks steeped in mystical scenery and history from times when Mary Queen of Scots and the Royal Stuarts used Falkland for retreats. The Lodge is also within walking distance of our local organic shop and café making us an ideal destination for those interested in healthy living. The Burgh Lodge is guaranteed to leave you feeling rejuvenated and ready to face everyday life.
£11/person first night £10/person thereafter, family and larger group discounts; favourable rates for booking entire lodge. Individual self catering, full catering for groups if booked in advance. Additional indoor space for larger group meetings is available close by.

Suitability or Specialism
Welcomes Everyone!

Isle of Erraid

http://www.erraid.com

A small tidal island off the Ross of Mull near Iona, Erraid has been in the care of the Findhorn Foundation since 1978. The houses (formerly lighthouse keepers' cottages), outbuildings and gardens are home to a small resident group and domestic animals. Our lives and rhythms are very close to the earth, the sea, the tides, the elements and the seasons. Our intention is to consciously embrace Spirit and to live as sustainably as we can, in harmony with nature. We do not adhere to nor exclude any creed or religion and welcome you to the community whatever your previous spiritual involvement. The emphasis is on "living education" and there are great opportunities for learning and growth as you work with us in the garden, kitchen or candle studio, or with maintenance and animals. Shared accommodation is in single or twin rooms, meals are predominantly vegetarian. There is hot and cold water and electricity, but the lavatories are outside earth closets.

Subject Specialities
Food & gardening, meditation.
Suitability or Specialism
Adults, couples, families with children.

Paul Johnson
Isle of Erraid
Fionnphort
Isle of Mull
Argyll
PA66 6BN

℡ 01681 700384

paul@erraid.fslife.co.uk

✔ **Own Course Programme**

12 bedspaces.

Special diets.

Focus New Age

Scotland/Isle of Mull

Findhorn Foundation

🌐 http://www.findhorn.org

Eva Ward
Findhorn Foundation
The Park, Findhorn
Forres
Morayshire
IV36 3TZ

✆ 01309 690311
✉ 01309 691301
✎ enquiries@findhorn.org

✔ **Own Course Programme**

⛺ 130 bedspaces.
🍽 Exclusively vegetarian.
🚗 Flights are available to Inverness or Aberdeen then train or bus to Forres then taxi to Cluny or The Park.

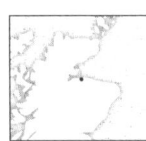

Focus Non denominational

The Findhorn Foundation is the educational and organisational cornerstone of the Findhorn Community, founded in 1962. We are an international centre of spiritual education and personal transformation and a daring experiment in how to live sustainably and in harmony with all of life. Life is rich and challenging as we seek to expand human consciousness through planetary service, cocreation with nature and acknowledging the divinity within all beings. We have two campuses, Cluny Hill College and The Park, and a retreat centre on the island of Iona. We welcome 14,000 visitors a year to tours, workshops and conferences and continue to develop our ecovillage at The Park as a positive and practical way to live sustainably on the earth.

The Findhorn Foundation is an NGO of the United Nations and the Ecovillage Project has been awarded "Best Practice" designation by the United Nations Centre for Human Settlements.

Event Types
Guided group retreats, own course programme, accredited courses.

Subject Specialities
Alternative lifestyles & technology, meditation, food & gardening, health & healing, self expression, arts & crafts, inner process, group process, conservation work, prayer.

Suitability or Specialism
Adults, lesbian women, gay men, young people 12 to 17, older people.

Eco-tourism features
Founding member of the Global Ecovillage Network, organic gardening, windmill, biological sewage treatment plant, recycling, high specification ecohouses, reforestation. Winner of the Green Tourism Business Scheme Gold Award.

Scotland/Morayshire

http://www.glengormcastle.co.uk

Glengorm Castle

Glengorm Castle stands on a headland on the north coast of the Isle of Mull within 5000 acres of rolling hills, heather and forests. Beyond the rocky coastline is the Atlantic Ocean with the Outer Hebrides on the horizon. Guests are encouraged to roam the estate, whether it is down to the coast or up to Loch an s'Airde Beinn volcano, there is a huge expanse in which to be alone.

Glengorm Coffee Shop
We have recently opened an art centre and coffee shop and these facilities are ideal for running workshops. Glengorm has its own market garden and organically run farm of highland cattle and blackface sheep. Food is direct from the estate or sourced locally using the highest quality and sustainable sources. Exhibitions are changed monthly through the summer in the main gallery with other artists exhibiting work in the coffee shop itself. Mull and Glengorm in particular has been a very popular area for landscape artists, musicians and writers. The gallery and coffee shop now provide a focus for local art and events. This venue can also be used for one day or longer for workshops, particularly outside the summer months when the island returns to a quieter state for those coming for contemplation and relaxation.

Self-Catering and B&B
The estate has 8 cottages and 2 flats within the castle, each with their own setting and character. The 5 B&B rooms are within the main Castle with 3 of the rooms looking out over the Atlantic. It is perfectly situated for the long summer nights and dramatic West Highland sunsets. All B&B rooms have en-suite bathrooms except for 1 which has its own adjacent private bathroom. Please look at the website for more details and photographs. People wishing to organise workshop weeks will need to arrange block bookings of accommodation well in advance.

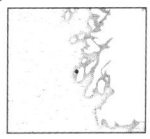

Fiona Noble
Glengorm Castle, Tobermory
Isle of Mull PA75 6QE
✆ 01688 302321
📠 01688 302738
✉ enquiries@glengormcastle.co.uk
✔ **Bed & Breakfast**
✔ **Venue for hire**

⌂ Castle has 5 B&B rooms (2 can be made into twin rooms) accommodating up to 10. Two flats in the castle can also accommodate 5 and 6 people each, additional accommodation in 8 estate cottages.
🍽 All catering in-house, resident chef, local ingredients.
♿ No wheelchair access
🚌 Buses and trains to Oban from Glasgow: 3 hours. Oban to Mull ferry 45 minutes. Craignure to Tobermory bus: 45 minutes. Taxi last 4 miles to castle. Collection arranged in special circumstances.

Scotland/Isle of Mull

Laurieston Hall

Jude Till
Laurieston Hall
Laurieston
Castle Douglas
Dumfries and Galloway
DG7 2NB

✓ **Retreat House**
✓ **Own Course Programme**
✓ **Venue for hire**

group full board (from £22), large indoor space, several small spaces

🛏 60 bedspaces (5 doubles, 5 family rooms), camping (20), no smoking indoors.

🍽 Vegetarian, special diets by request.

♿ Wheelchair access.

🚌 Bus from Dumfries to Castle Douglas. We arrange pick-ups in Castle Douglas - 7 miles away.

Intentional community (established 1972) in secluded, rural area, 12 miles from the Solway coast. 30 people, aged 1 - 70, maintain large property, walled vegetable garden, livestock and 123 acres of woodland. Private lochside beach. Wood-fired sauna, campfire, and large pond at the bottom of extensive lawn. Volleyball, croquet, table-tennis and snooker. Camping. House band provides ceilidh/circle dance.
We host week-long events from April to September for organised groups. Some holiday and building/gardening/maintenance weeks are run by the resident community. Wide range of interests, and open to new events. Minimum booking(s): 15. Visitors join with residents in supervised work-sharing in kitchens, wood gathering or cleaning tasks.
Annual newsletter out January describes both the housing co-operative community and the People Centre programme. Write enclosing two first class stamps for brochure. Not open for B&B.

Event Types
Self directed retreats, own course programme, working holidays.

Subject Specialities
Alternative lifestyles & technology, music & dance, group process, self expression, body & breathwork, conservation

work, food & gardening.

Suitability or Specialism
Adults(+), families with children(+), lesbian women, gay men(+), young people 12 to 17, children under 12(+).

Eco-tourism features
Collective ownership and work allocation, hydroelectric system, oakwood conservation, re-cycling.

http://www.newboldhouse.org

NewBold House

NewBold House is a working spiritual community which welcomes guests to join in community life and educational workshops. It offers an integrated experience of living and relating in a different way. The atmosphere created in this beautiful old mansion house and its seven acres of woodland and gardens provides a caring and nurturing environment for individual self-exploration and growth.

Event Types
Self directed retreats.

Suitability or Specialism
Adults.

Tom
NewBold House
St Leonards Road
Forres
Morayshire
IV36 2RE

✆ 01309 672659
✉ newbold@findhorn.org

✓ **Retreat House**
✓ **Own Course Programme**

🛏 30 bedspaces (1 single.)
🍽 Exclusively vegetarian.

Focus New Age

Scotland/Morayshire

Shanti Griha

🌟 http://www.shantigriha.com

Brian & Kathrin Cooper
Shanti Griha
Scoraig Peninsula
Dundonnell, Garve
Ross and Cromarty
IV23 2RE
✆ 01854 633260
✉ shantigriha@hotmail.com

✔ **Retreat House**
✔ **Own Course Programme**
✔ **Venue for hire**
group full board (£30), large indoor space
🛏 10 bedspaces (4 single, 1 double, 1 family room.)
🍽 Exclusively vegetarian, special diets.
♿ None.
🚌 Bus to Ullapool, pick up by arrangement.

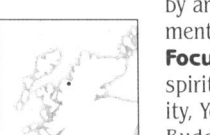

Focus Eco-spirituality, Yogic, Buddhist

Scoraig Peninsula in Northwest Scotland, one of the remotest places on the British mainland, can only be reached on foot or by boat. Shanti Griha, House of Peace, is a lovingly restored and extended croft house set in two acres of magic garden, with water coming from a spring and electricity from a windmill. The house is situated at the foot of Ben Ghobhlach and looks out onto Little Loch Broom and the open sea towards the Outer Hebrides. The Highland wilderness offers walks and wildlife such as otters, seals, red deer and wild goats. Brian Cooper, Director of the Edinburgh Astanga Yoga Centre, holds regular workshops in Yoga and Thai Massage. Kathrin Cooper, who has a Buddhist family background, teaches Meditation, Buddhism and Tai Ji. Further workshops include windpower, art and creative writing. Please ask for our brochure. Shanti Griha features a large and bright meditation room and is open for groups and individual retreats.

Event Types
Guided group retreats, guided individual retreats, self directed retreats, own course programme, teacher training.
Subject Specialities
Alternative lifestyles & technology.
Suitability or Specialism
Adults.
Eco-tourism features
Own windmill, own spring, locally sourced organic food and own vegetable garden, herb garden and orchard.

Other Places and Organisations

Avalon
Elphin
Lairg
Sutherland
IV27 4HH
Bed & Breakfast
✆ 01854 666204

Avingormack Guesthouse and Retreats
Boat of Garten
Inverness-shire
PH24 3BT
Retreat House

The Bield at Blackruthven
Tibbermore
Perth
PH1 1PY
Retreat House
✆ 01738 583238

Bishop's House
Isle of Iona
Argyll
PA76 6SJ
Retreat House

Carberry
Musselburgh
Midlothian
EH21 8PY
Venue for Hire

Centre of Light
Tighnabruaich
Struy
Beauly
Inverness-shire
IV4 7JU
Retreat House

Choraidh Croft Farm
94 Laid
Loch Enbollside
Altnaharra
Lairg
Sutherland
IV27 4UN
Bed & Breakfast

Dod Mill Retreat Centre
Dod Mill House
Lauder
Berwickshire
TD2 6SE
Venue for Hire

Other Places and Organisations

Great Glen Holidays
Torlundy
Fort William
Inverness-shire
PH33 6SW
Venue for Hire

Jenny's Bothy
Dellachuper
Corgarff
Strathdon
Aberdeenshire
AB36 8YP
Venue for Hire

Pluscarden Abbey
Pluscarden
Elgin
Morayshire
IV30 3UA
Retreat House

Quiraing Lodge
Staffin
Portree
Isle of Skye
IV51 9JS
Own Course Programme

Rhanich Sheep Farm
The Rhanich
Edderton
Tain
Ross and Cromarty
IV19 1LG
Bed & Breakfast

St Columba Hotel
Isle of Iona
Argyll
PA76 6SL
Bed & Breakfast

Other Places and Organisations

Salisbury Centre
2 Salisbury Road
Edinburgh
EH16 5AB
Own Course Programme

Samye Ling Tibetan Centre
Eskdalemuir
Dumfries and Galloway
DG13 0QL
Own Course Programme

Tabor Trust Retreat Centre
Key House
High Street
Falkland
Fife
KY7 7BU
Retreat House

Tigh a Gharraidh
Acharn
Aberfeldy
Perthshire
PH15 2HP
Bed & Breakfast
✆ 01887 829678

Whitchester Christian Guest House & Retreat Centre
Borthaugh
Hawick
Roxburghshire
TD9 7LN
Retreat House

Woodwick House
Evie
Orkney
KW17 2PQ
Bed & Breakfast

North of England

Venues in
Cheshire
Cumbria
East Yorkshire
Isle of Man
Merseyside
North Yorkshire
Northumberland
West Yorkshire

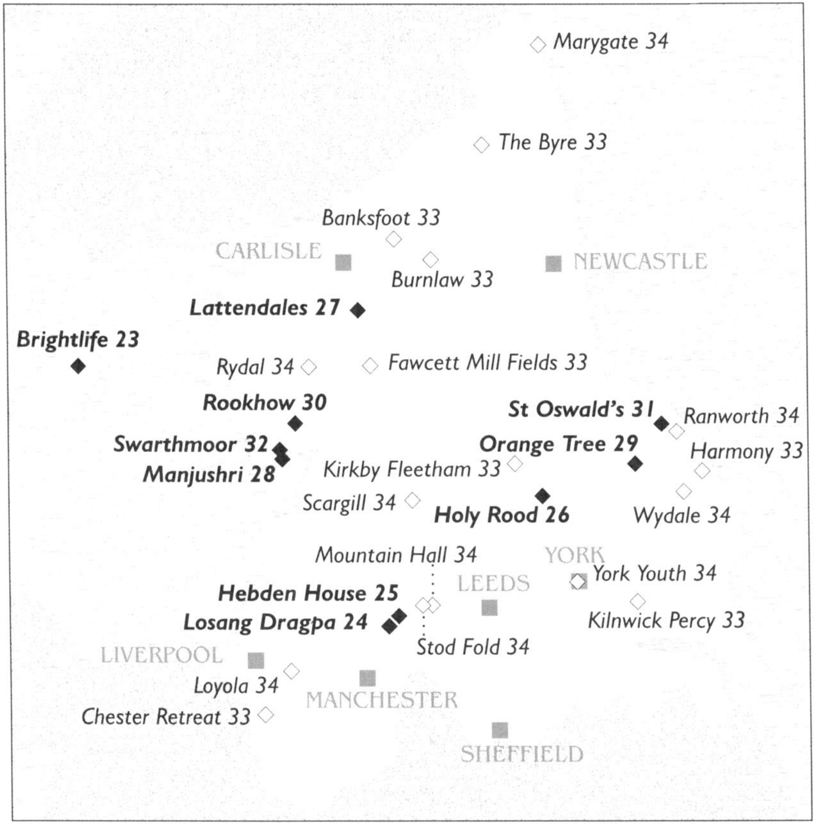

Places to BE 2004/Page 22

◇ Marygate 34

◇ The Byre 33

Banksfoot 33 ◇

CARLISLE ■   ■ NEWCASTLE

◇ Burnlaw 33

Lattendales 27 ◆

Brightlife 23 ◆

Rydal 34 ◇   ◇ Fawcett Mill Fields 33

Rookhow 30 ◆   **St Oswald's 31** ◆   Ranworth 34 ◇

Swarthmoor 32 ◆   **Orange Tree 29** ◆   Harmony 33 ◇

Manjushri 28 ◆   Kirkby Fleetham 33 ◇

Scargill 34 ◇   **Holy Rood 26** ◆   Wydale 34 ◇

Mountain Hall 34   YORK
Hebden House 25 ◆   LEEDS   ◇ York Youth 34
Losang Dragpa 24 ◆   ◇ Kilnwick Percy 33
Stod Fold 34

LIVERPOOL ■
Loyola 34 ◇
Chester Retreat 33 ◇   MANCHESTER ■

■ SHEFFIELD

http://www.brightlife.com

Brightlife

Relax in luxury and discover hidden talents with weekend courses at Brightlife.
At the heart of the British Isles, the Isle of Man is an Island steeped in history and rich in Heritage, a mystical place to relax in luxury, enjoy gourmet cuisine and discover hidden talents with weekend workshops and week-long retreats at Brightlife. Set in seclusion and surrounded by the beauties of nature, Brightlife offers you the chance to relax and recharge. There is a unique library of books on personal and spiritual development, also a floatation suite and BETAR music therapy room.

Brightlife Conferencing offers a bespoke service tailored to your requirements, with the emphasis on attention to detail.

Event Types
Guided group weekend retreats, Business retreats.

Subject Specialities
Personal development, health & healing, spiritual awareness.

Jane Gibson, Centre Manager
Brightlife
Ballalheaney
Andreas Road
Andreas
Isle of Man
IM7 4EN

℃ 01624 880318
℡ 01624 880967
✉ brightlife@brightlife.com

✓ **Retreat House**
✓ **Own Course Programme**
✓ **Venue for hire**

↵ 10 double/single rooms, Five diamond, gold crown luxury
🍽 gourmet cuisine
♿ one bedroom disabled adapted
✈ 35 minutes plane ride from Liverpool

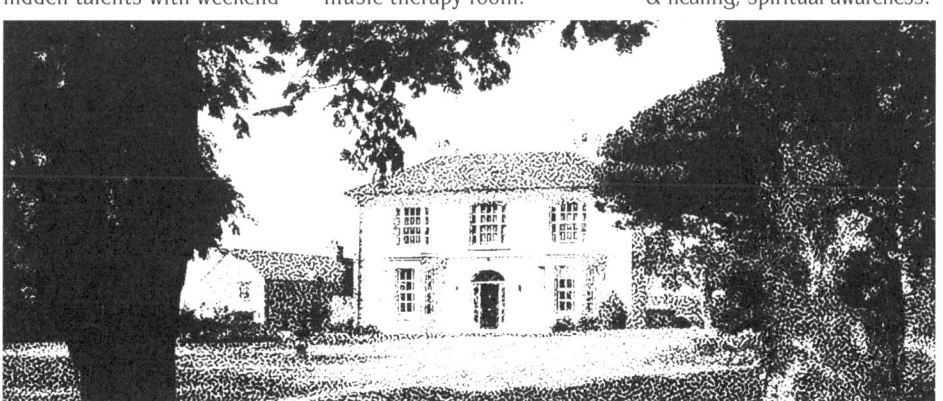

Losang Dragpa Buddhist Centre

🕸 http://www.losangdragpa.com

Chris Snow
Dobroyd Castle
Pexwood Road
Todmorden
OL14 7JJ

✆ 01706 812247 x201
✆ 01706 818901
✎ info@losangdragpa.com
✔ **Retreat House**
✔ **Bed & Breakfast**
✔ **Own Course Programme**
🛏 44 bedspaces (12 singles, 2 twins, 2 doubles, 2 family rooms, 2 dormitories).
🍽 Exclusively vegetarian, special diets.
🚶 within walking distance

Focus Buddhist

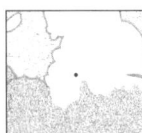

Losang Dragpa Centre is a residential Buddhist College that attracts an international community of about 35 people, both lay and ordained, male and female from all walks of life. It is beautifully set in a Victorian castle in the Yorkshire Pennines overlooking the Calder Valley. With a Peace Garden, World Peace Café and Gift Shop adding to the tranquillity of the surrounding countryside. As a meditation centre, we offer organised study programmes as well as day courses and weekend meditation breaks for the general public. We offer a B&B option called Build-Your-Own Break. If visitors would like to learn more about meditation we can provide them with an experienced meditation teacher who can assist you in your meditation practice. Or if you just need a quiet break, we can make that happen as well. You tell us what you need and we'll arrange it.

We are also a facility for inner peace teaching people to transform destructive states of mind (such as stress and anger) into peaceful ones (like loving-kindness and compassion). Everybody – regardless of religion or background. Try sampling life in a friendly Buddhist community on a working holiday, where you get delicious vegetarian meals and accommodation in exchange for 35 hours work per week. We also offer guided group retreats, day courses, guided weekend meditation breaks, self directed retreats, study course programmes, teacher training, working holidays.

Subject Specialities
Buddhism, meditation, prayer.

Suitability or Specialism
Adults(++), couples, families with children, women, men, young people 12 to 17, children under 12, older people.

North of England/West Yorkshire

Hebden House

🌐 http://www.hebden-house.co.uk

Set in two acres of woodland, Hebden House offers a peaceful and secluded setting from which to run courses, workshops, seminars and retreats. Hebden House offers 58 beds in 15 en-suite rooms. Bed linen service is provided. Seminar room for up to 50, plus break-out room and kitchenette, pleasant outlook onto a sheltered courtyard. There is an Additional Conference Area available for up to 400 people. Catering is vegetarian and is provided by Jim and Ash from "Laughing Gravy". Vegan food a speciality of the chefs. Other diets easily catered for. Separate dining room seats 58. Disabled toilets and Stannah lifts to all levels. Youth groups must be supervised.

Event Types
Self directed retreats, business retreats.

Suitability or Specialism
Adults, young people 12 to 17, children under 12

Lynn Prior
The Birchcliffe Centre
Birchcliffe Road
Hebden Bridge
West Yorkshire
HX7 8DG
✆ 01422 843626
📠 01422 843648
✉ enqs@hebden-house.co.uk

✔ **Venue for hire**
group full board (£35 to £42.50), large indoor space, several small spaces

🛏 58 bedspaces (15 singles, 1 twin, 15 family rooms).
🍽 Exclusively vegetarian, special diets.
♿ Wheelchair access.
🚆 Train station and bus 5 to 10 minutes on foot.

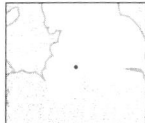

North of England/West Yorkshire

Holy Rood House

http://www.holyroodhouse.freeuk.com

Rev Elizabeth Baxter
Holy Rood House
Centre for Health & Pastoral Care
10 Sowerby Road, Thirsk
North Yorkshire YO7 1HX
✆ 01845 522580
✉ holyroodhouse@
centrethirsk.fsnet.co.uk

✔ **Retreat House**
✔ **Own Course Programme**
✔ **Venue for hire**

group full board (up to £37), large indoor space, several small spaces

🛏 22 bedspaces (6 singles, 6 twins, 2 doubles).
🍽 Special diets.
♿ Ramps to both houses. Not suitable for someone in a wheelchair permanently.
🚆 Train to Thirsk or coach to Market Place, Thirsk.

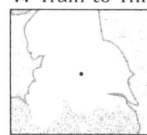

Focus
Radical Christian

Overlooking the Hambledon Hills, Holy Rood House is a safe and creative space, offering therapeutic support at a time of need, and a gentle place for someone looking for a retreat with a difference. The relaxed, creative and welcoming environment of the House creates opportunity for people of all ages to find empowerment towards their own healing and well-being. With professional counsellors, therapists, creative artists and spiritual directors available to accompany guests on their therapeutic and spiritual journeys, many people find Holy Rood House a unique and special place, and discover the extraordinary within the ordinary of daily life and rhythm of the residential community, and those who support the life of the House day by day.

Holy Rood House is committed to working in areas of anger and stress management, mediation and conflict resolution, body spirituality, mental health and caring for the carers, and has a particular rapport with young people. The vitality and friendship of the community, the animals and gardens, and beauty of our surroundings, a reputation for excellent home-made food and comfortable rooms, all create a sense of well-being and belonging, where pain and trauma is held tenderly, laughter is infectious, and personal integrity and life-style is respected while we celebrate the richness and adventure of difference. Together we work towards justice and peace within an ecological awareness, and this is reflected in the original liturgies celebrated in the chapel.

Arising out of the work of Holy Rood House, The Centre for The Study of Theology and Health offers conference and research opportunities to explore the interface between theology and health with a radical agenda, shaped by all we learn together through the work of Holy Rood House, and by all who offer their thoughts and ideas.

Lattendales

🏠 http://www.lattendales.info

The Friends Fellowship of Healing was formed in 1935 by some members of the Religious Society of Friends (Quakers). The Fellowship believes that God's purpose for humankind is wholeness of body, mind and spirit. It facilitates a number of activities to help people towards achieving this 'wholeness'. The function of Lattendales is to provide a sanctuary or retreat for those who feel in need of rest, whether spiritually, mentally or physically.

Lattendales is run in accordance with the principles of the Religious Society of Friends, but welcomes everyone irrespective of their religious beliefs.

The house is open from March to November, and guests are invited to enjoy the peaceful atmosphere of Lattendales and its beautitul formal gardens.

Event Types
Self directed retreats.

Subject Specialities
Health & healing, meditation, prayer.

Suitability or Specialism
Adults, couples, women, men, young people 12 to 17, older people.

John & Vivien Cran
Lattendales
Berrier Road
Greystoke
Penrith, Cumbria
CA11 0UE
✆ 01768 483229
📠 01768 483058
✉ wardens@lattendales.info

✔ **Retreat House**
✔ **Own Course Programme**
✔ **Venue for hire**

group full board (£38 to £41), group self catering (£24), large indoor space

🛏 21 bedspaces (5 singles, 7 twins, 1 double).
🍽 Special diets.
♿ 1 twin-bedded room, own toilet.
🚍 Penrith Station then bus or taxi (5 miles)

Focus
Quaker/Open

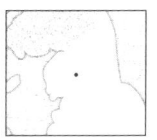

Manjushri Kadampa Meditation Centre

http://www.manjushri.org

Kelsang Namgyal
Conishead Priory
Ulverston
Cumbria
LA12 9QQ

✆ 01229 584029
✆ 01229 584029
✉ info@manjushri.org

✓ **Retreat House**
✓ **Own Course Programme**

🍽 Exclusively vegetarian.

Focus Buddhist

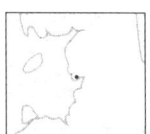

Manjushri Kadampa Meditation Centre, based at Conishead Priory in Ulverston, provides an inspiring and peaceful environment in which people can learn about Buddhism and meditation.
Manjushri Centre offers a wide variety of courses on meditation and Buddhist practices which are suitable for everyone, from those who seek simple relaxation to those who wish to find lasting inner peace and contentment through following the Buddhist path.
In the grounds of Manjushri Centre is the beautiful Kadampa World Peace Temple, which was built by the Buddhist community to prove a place for quiet reflection and spiritual inspiration. Prayers are held daily in the Temple as well as regular weekend courses. Just south of the Lake District, Conishead Priory is beautifully situated in many acres of woodland and gardens on the shores of Morecambe Bay. The beach is only a five minute walk from the Priory through mature woodland which provides a quiet and reflective environment.
If you would like to find out more about Manjushri Centre and the courses and study programmes we offer, or would like to do a working visit and spend time as part of our community please call or visit our website.

The Orange Tree

🕸 http://www.theorangetree.com

The Orange Tree - where relaxation comes naturally! The Orange Tree is a family run "Relaxation Centre" situated in a beautiful, tranquil location in Rosedale, deep in the heart of the North Yorkshire Moors. We run residential "Relaxation Workshops" accommodating up to 15 people, combining great food (vegi) and wine with four relaxation sessions, aromatherapy massage, sauna and lovely walks.

Our rooms are all comfortably furnished and all have their own facilities and we encourage informality as well as allowing everyone choices to participate or not.

We will accept bookings from 1 to 15 people and can also hire out the complete facility, or modify our own programme to suit. We charge £115 per person which includes two nights, all meals and relaxation demonstrations, based on sharing a twin bedded room.

Rob Davies
The Orange Tree
Rosedale Abbey, Rosedale East
Pickering, North Yorkshire
YO18 8RH
✆ 01751 417219
📠 01751 417219
✉ relax@theorangetree.com

✔ **Retreat House**
✔ **Holiday Operator**
✔ **Own Course Programme**
✔ **Venue for hire**

group full board (£75 to £100), large indoor space

🛏 15 bedspaces (1 single, 7 twins, 1 double, 1 triple).
🍴 Exclusively vegetarian, special diets.
♿ Wheelchair access.
🚌 Nearest bus station - Pickering, then taxi (20 minutes). Nearest railway station - Malton, then taxi (35 minutes).

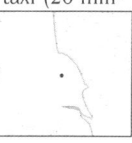

Rookhow Centre

Robert Straughton
Rookhow Centre
Rusland
Ulverston
Cumbria
LA12 8LA

✆ 01229 860231
✆ 01229 860231
✉ rookhow@britishlibrary.net

✔ **Retreat House**
✔ **Venue for hire**

⌕ 20 bedspaces (2 doubles, 1 family room, 2 dormitories).
🚌 Train to Ulverston then Postbus to the door, Monday to Saturday.

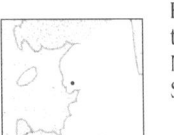

Focus Quaker (all welcome)

Perhaps the most beautifully situated budget accommodation in the Lake District; in 14 acres of peaceful woodland, between Lakes Coniston and Windermere. By Grizedale Forest, with its sculpture and trails. Stunning walking/biking country. Rookhow is an early 'Quaker' or 'Friends' Meeting House. The 'Centre' provides accommodation in the former stables. Self-catering, though catering can sometimes be arranged. The Meeting House, in use since 1725, is available separately for conferences, workshops, seminars, dance, yoga etc. Open to those of all denominations or of none. Bedspaces from £8.50 per person per night, children half price. Thirty bedspaces with bedrolls in the Meeting House. Spiritual retreats of all kinds.

Event Types
Guided group retreats, self directed retreats, business retreats, working holidays.
Subject Specialities
Arts & crafts, conservation work, outdoor activities & sport, body & breathwork, meditation.
Eco-tourism features
Yurt accommodation created in 2002. 12 acres of woods managed ecologically.

http://www.ohpwhitby.org

St Oswald's Pastoral Centre

St Oswald's Pastoral Centre is run by four Sisters of the Anglican Order of the Holy Paraclete. Within the context of our regular rhythm of prayer and worship, we offer hospitality to individuals or small groups for retreat, rest or quiet. The Centre is situated in its own grounds overlooking the Esk valley and the North York Moors. It is an ideal centre for those who enjoy walking and is three miles from the historic port and town of Whitby with its Abbey ruins and picturesque harbour. Guests are welcome to join the Sisters for services and Sisters are available if anyone wants a listening ear or some guidance on making a retreat.

The Grimston Room is a large (maximum 40) conference room which is available for day groups. The Centre runs a programme of events through the year.
Normally the Centre is closed on Sunday nights.

Event Types
Guided group retreats, guided individual retreats, self directed retreats, own course programme.

Subject Specialities
Prayer.

Suitability or Specialism
Adults, couples, older people.

Sister in Charge
St Oswald's Pastoral Centre
Woodlands Drive
Sleights, Whitby
North Yorkshire YO21 1RY
℡ 01947 810496
℻ 01947 810750
✉ ohpstos@globalnet.co.uk
✔ **Retreat House**
✔ **Own Course Programme**
✔ **Venue for hire**
group full board (£35), large indoor & several small spaces
⛏ 17 bedspaces (10 singles, 3 twins).
🍽 Special diets.
♿ Limited wheelchair access.
🚆 Train to Sleights Station or coach from York to Sleights Bridge. 15 minute walk or we can meet you if requested.
Focus Christian

North of England/North Yorkshire

Swarthmoor Hall

🔖 http://www.swarthmoorhall.co.uk

Steven Deeming
Swarthmoor Hall
Ulverston
Cumbria
LA12 0JQ

☎ 01229 583204
✆ 01229 583283
✉ swarthmrhall@gn.apc.org

✔ **Own Course Programme**
✔ **Venue for hire**

⌇ 16 bedspaces (4 singles, 6 twins).
🍽 Special diets.
♿ Wheelchair access.
🚂 Ulverston Station then 5 minute taxi ride or 15 minute walk along road or well-marked footpath

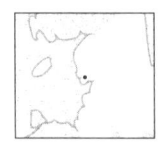

Focus Quaker

Built circa 1586, this Grade II* listed Hall is a centre for retreat programmes, day-workshops and self-catering holidays in beautiful South Lakeland. Visitors enjoy our peaceful gardens and wild flower meadow. The Hall itself holds one of the finest collections of 17th century furniture in the North West, and is associated with the early Quaker movement.

Holiday accommodation is in two flats in the Hall, and one (wheelchair friendly) in the Fell Barn. These can be used as one whole unit of 16 beds, or separately as three self-catering units of 5(+1), 5 (+1), and 4 bed spaces. Meeting and seminar rooms include historic rooms in the Hall, and a meeting and dining area for 30 people. OHP, slide projector, TVs and VCRs available.

Shops, cafes and restaurants can be found in the market town of Ulverston – 1.7 miles by road, or by footpath across fields and public access woodland.

Event Types
Guided group retreats, own course programme.

Subject Specialities
Group process, inner process, prayer.

Suitability or Specialism
Adults, families with children, lesbian women, gay men, women, older people.

Other Places and Organisations

Beds@Banksfoot
Banksfoot Farm
Brampton
Cumbria
CA8 2JH
Bed & Breakfast
℅ 016977 42427
✉ beds@banksfoot.fsnet.co.uk

Burnlaw Healing and Retreat Centre
Burnlaw
Whitfield
Northumberland
NE47 8HF
Retreat House

The Byre Vegetarian B&B
Harbottle
Morpeth
Northumberland
NE65 7DG
Bed & Breakfast

Chester Retreat House
11 Abbey Square
Chester
Cheshire
CH1 2HU
Retreat House

Fawcett Mill Fields
Gaisgill
Tebay
Penrith
Cumbria
CA10 3UB
Venue for Hire

Harmony Country Lodge
Limestone Road
Burniston
Scarborough
North Yorkshire
YO13 0DG
Retreat House
℅ 0800 298 5840

Kilnwick Percy Hall
Kilnwick Percy Hall
Pocklington
York
YO4 2UF
Own Course Programme

Kirkby Fleetham Hall
Kirkby Fleetham
Northallerton
DL7 0SU

Venue for Hire

Other Places and Organisations

Loyola Hall
Warrington Road
Rainhill
Prescot
Merseyside
L35 6NZ
Retreat House

Marygate House
Holy Island
Berwick-upon-Tweed
Northumberland
TD15 2SD
Retreat House

Mountain Hall Centre
Brighouse & Denholme Road
Queensbury
Bradford
West Yorkshire
BD13 1LH
Own Course Programme

Ranworth Vegetarian Guesthouse
Ranworth
Church Road
Ravenscar
Scarborough
North Yorkshire
YO13 0LZ
Bed & Breakfast

Rydal Hall
Ambleside
Cumbria
LA22 9LX
Retreat House

Scargill House
Kettlewell
Skipton
North Yorkshire
BD23 5HU
Venue for Hire

Stod Fold Barn
Stod Fold
Ogden
Halifax
West Yorkshire
HX2 8XL
Venue for Hire
© 01422 244854

Wydale Hall
Wydale Lane
Brompton by Sawdon
Scarborough
North Yorkshire
YO13 9DG
Venue for Hire

York Youth Hotel
11/13 Bishophill Senior
York
YO1 6EF
Bed & Breakfast

East of England

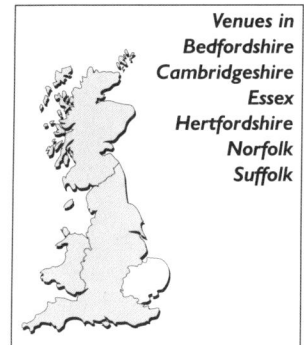

Venues in
Bedfordshire
Cambridgeshire
Essex
Hertfordshire
Norfolk
Suffolk

Voewood 37 ◆
◇ Wood Norton Hall 39
◇ NORWICH
Old Red Lion 39
◇ All Hallows 38
◇ Bishop Woodford House 38
Houghton Chapel 39
◇ Turvey Abbey 39   Burwell 38   ◇ Vajrasana 39
◇ Ickwell Bury 39   CAMBRIDGE
■ LUTON   **Marshwinds 36** ◆
Amaravati 38
◇ All Saints 38   ◇ Arthur Findlay 38

◇ Bradwell Othona 38

Marshwinds

http://www.marshwinds.co.uk

Tom Southern
32 Saxmundham Road
Aldeburgh
Suffolk
IP15 5JE

✆ 01728 452695

✓ **Bed & Breakfast**

3 bedspaces (1 single, 1 double.)
Exclusively vegetarian, special diets.

🚆 Trains from Ipswich, Norwich or London to Saxmundham or Woodbridge then bus to Aldeburgh

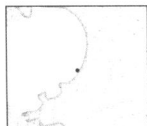

Marshwinds is in the small seaside town of Aldeburgh, a town known internationally for the annual Aldeburgh Festival. There is music throughout the year, both in the town and in the nearby Maltings at Snape as well as annual literary, poetry, jazz and documentary film festivals. Aldeburgh also offers miles of shingle beach to stroll along as well as inland walks. Even in high summer the local lanes are never busy; the sandy rolling landscape, with gorse, bracken and pine trees and banks of reeds along the many rivers, encourages you to slow down.

We came to Aldeburgh in 2001 to get away from the stressful pressure of city life. Marshwinds, designed and decorated in a simple modern style, is our peaceful retreat. We share with guests a collection of contemporary prints, photographs, modern ceramics and wooden artefacts that are displayed around the house. We have a long, south facing, garden which guests are welcome to use. We plan to build a garden pavilion in the coming year for meditation and quiet reflection.

Two guest rooms: a single and a double, each with its own shower room. A hearty, mainly organic, vegetarian breakfast is served. We can provide suppers and packed lunch to order. Non-smoking. Off road parking.

Suitability or Specialism
Adults, couples, lesbian women, gay men, women, men.

Voewood

http://www.voewood.com

Voewood is a magical house with a very special, unique atmosphere set in beautiful Grade 1 listed gardens and situated five miles from the stunning North Norfolk coastline including Morston, Cley, Blakeney and Stifkey. The breathtaking expanse of Holkham beach is a 25 minute drive and the charming Georgian Town of Holt is just one mile up the road. Voewood was built by E S Prior for Percy Lloyd between 1903 and 1905 and is known as one of the finest houses of the Art and Crafts movement. The redecoration has been done to remain true to Prior's vision while interpreting it in a modern idiom. Voewood is ideal for yoga retreats, teachers' training courses and holistic workshops and can be booked for both weekend and weekly retreats throughout the year. It is also available for house party bookings so you can relax with all your friends in this spacious and intriguing home. The large and well equipped kitchen means you are free to do your own catering or we can provide a caterer for you. During the summer months, a Tepee is erected in the garden so you can build your own fire and sleep outside to be closer to the stars!

Rebecca Laurence
Voewood
Cromer Road
High Kelling
Holt
Norfolk
NR25 6QS
☏ 020 7499 0974
✆ 020 7499 0799
✉ rebecca@simonfinch.com
✔ **Retreat House**
✔ **Venue for hire**

⌨ 30 bedspaces (1 single, 5 twins, 7 doubles, 1 dormitory).
🍽 Special diets.
🚂 Pay train from Norwich to Sheringham then local taxi to Voewood (20 minutes). Own transport advisable.

Focus All embracing

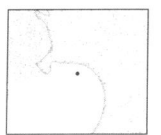

East of England/Norfolk

Places to BE 2004/Page 37

Other Places and Organisations

Community of All Hallows
All Hallows Convent
Belsey Bridge Road
Ditchingham
Bungay
Suffolk
NR25 2DT

Retreat House
© 01986 892749

Amaravati Buddhist Centre
Great Gaddesden
Hemel Hempstead
Hertfordshire
HP1 3BZ
Retreat House

The Arthur Findlay College
Stansted Hall
Church Road
Burton End
Stansted
Essex
CM24 8UD
Own Course Programme

Bishop Woodford House
Barton Road
Ely
Cambridgeshire
CB7 4DX
Retreat House

Bradwell Othona Community
East Hall Farm
East End Road
Bradwell on Sea
Southminster
Essex
CM0 7PN
Retreat House

All Saints Pastoral Centre
London Colney
St Albans
Hertfordshire
AL2 1AF
Retreat House

Burwell House
North Street
Burwell
Cambridge
CB5 0BA
Venue for Hire

Other Places and Organisations

Houghton Chapel Centre
Church View
Chapel Lane
Houghton
Huntingdon
Cambridgeshire
PE17 2AY
Venue for Hire

The Old Red Lion
Bailey Street
Castle Acre
Kings Lynn
Norfolk
PE32 2AG
Bed & Breakfast

Vajrasana Retreat Centre
care of London Buddhist
Centre
51 Roman Road
Bethnal Green
London
E2 0HU
Own Course Programme

Ickwell Bury
Biggleswade
Bedfordshire
SG18 9EF
Own Course Programme

Turvey Abbey
Turvey
Bedford
MK43 8DE
Retreat House

Wood Norton Hall
Hall Lane
Wood Norton
Dereham
Norfolk
NR20 5BE
Venue for Hire

The Midlands

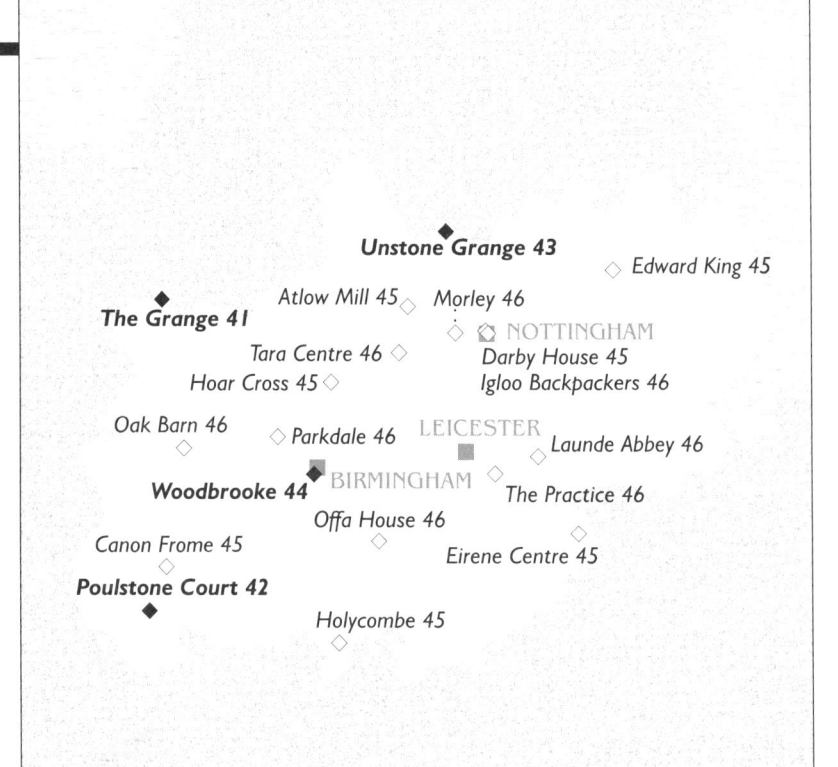

Venues in
Derbyshire
Herefordshire
Leicestershire
Lincolnshire
Northamptonshire
Nottinghamshire
Shropshire
Staffordshire
Warwickshire
West Midlands

Places to BE

- **Unstone Grange 43**
- Edward King 45
- Atlow Mill 45
- Morley 46
- **The Grange 41**
- NOTTINGHAM
- Tara Centre 46
- Darby House 45
- Hoar Cross 45
- Igloo Backpackers 46
- Oak Barn 46
- Parkdale 46
- LEICESTER
- Launde Abbey 46
- **Woodbrooke 44**
- BIRMINGHAM
- Offa House 46
- The Practice 46
- Canon Frome 45
- Eirene Centre 45
- **Poulstone Court 42**
- Holycombe 45

The Grange

🔸 http://www.thegrange.uk.com

Set in 10 beautiful acres of lawns, woodland, organic herb and vegetable gardens, and with light and large public lounges and library, there is plenty of scope at the Grange for individuals and groups to find their own quiet spaces and peaceful surroundings. We have our own programme of events that includes art and craft workshops, yoga, meditation, writing, and exploring the second half of life for women. We also take block bookings from groups looking for venues, and, at other times, offer bed and breakfast to individuals.

Believing that there are many routes to spiritual peace and fulfilment, we are open minded about the religious backgrounds, or not, of our guests welcoming all. The Grange is just outside the small town of Ellesmere, located in a wonderfully unspoilt region of north Shropshire, justly called the Shropshire lakeland, and is in striking distance of the magnificent Welsh borderlands.

Event Types
Guided group retreats, business retreats, own course programme.

Subject Specialities
Arts & crafts, body & breathwork, inner process, meditation, outdoor activities & sport, prayer, self expression.

Suitability or Specialism
Adults.

Rosie Ward-Allen
The Grange, Grange Road
Ellesmere, Shropshire
SY12 9DE
✆ 01691 623495
📠 01691 623227
✉ rosie@thegrange.uk.com

✔ **Bed & Breakfast**
✔ **Own Course Programme**
✔ **Venue for hire**

group full board (£43 to £53), large & several small spaces

🛏 25 bedspaces (5 singles, 4 twins, 4 doubles, 2 family rooms, most with en-suite bathrooms.)
🍽 Special diets.
♿ Wheelchair access.
🚌 Shrewsbury Station then bus or taxi (approximately 45 minutes travelling time)

Focus
Open-minded

The Midlands/Shropshire

Poulstone Court

🔗 http://www.poulstone.com

Marigold Farmer
Poulstone Court
Kings Caple
Hereford
HR1 4UA

📞 01432 840251
📠 01432 840860
✉ poulstone@btinternet.com

✔ **Venue for hire**

🛏 36 bedspaces.
🍽 Special diets.
🚆 Hereford railway station 6 miles.

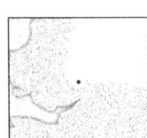

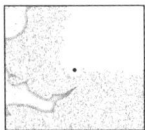

Poulstone Court, a spacious and comfortable Victorian country house, is a residential venue midway between Hereford and Ross-on-Wye. Five minutes' walk from the River Wye, it lies in lush, peaceful surroundings. The beautiful grounds include a walled garden and flat lawns perfect for outside activity. Sleeping accommodation is in attractive- ly furnished one- to five-bedded rooms, with a self-contained flat ideal for facilitators. Two large workshop spaces in the house are complemented by a spacious barn, perfect for movement. All food is vegetarian. Poulstone Court is regularly used for courses in Tai Chi, meditation, healing, counselling, shamanism, yoga and movement. We specialise in creating a clear, vibrant space consecrated to service, nourishment and support for the groups and courses that come here.

Event Types
Regeneration programmes.

Subject Specialities
Body & breathwork, health & healing, inner process, ritual & shamanic, meditation, T'ai chi, Yoga.

Suitability or Specialism
Adults.

Unstone Grange

http://www.unstonegrange.co.uk

A centre for personal creative growth. Set in the lovely Derbyshire countryside, the atmosphere at Unstone Grange attracts community and youth groups of all types. They come to use our centre to access and express their creative spirit through dance, drama, craftwork, writing, painting, music, meditation, bodywork, healing and a wide range of other activities. From £11 per person per night self catering.

Event Types
Guided group retreats, self directed retreats, working holidays.

Subject Specialities
Alternative lifestyles & technology, arts & crafts, body & breathwork, conservation work, counselling, earth mysteries, food & gardening, group process, health & healing, inner process, meditation, prayer, ritual & shamanic.

Suitability or Specialism
Adults.

Eco-tourism features
Over 2 acres of organic gardens and orchards. Soil Association certified.

Angela Barney
Unstone Grange
Crow Lane
Unstone
Dronfield
Derbyshire
S18 4AL

✆ 01246 412344
✆ 01246 412344
✉ admin@unstonegrange.co.uk

✔ **Venue for hire**

🛏 35 bedspaces (4 twins, 6 family rooms.)
🍴 Special diets.
🚆 Chesterfield Station 4 miles, take taxi or buses. Full details at website.

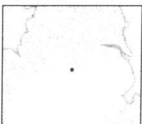

Focus Open

The Midlands/Derbyshire

Woodbrooke Quaker Study Centre

http://www.woodbrooke.org.uk

Fiona Sorotos
Woodbrooke
1046 Bristol Road
Birmingham
West Midlands
B29 6LJ

☏ 0121 472 5171
✆ 0121 472 5173
✉ enquiries@woodbrooke.org.uk

✔ **Own Course Programme**
✔ **Venue for hire**

🍽 Special diets.
🚌 Lots of regular buses from Birmingham New Street station or local train to Selly Oak.

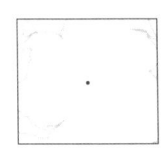

Focus Quaker

Woodbrooke Quaker Study Centre set in its own 10 acres of organically managed garden and grounds provides a refreshing oasis of calm in an urban setting. The house is a handsome Grade 2 listed building given to the Religious Society of Friends by George and Elizabeth Cadbury in 1903.

We provide comfortable and unpretentious hospitality as well as delicious food catering for a range of special diets. There are several meeting rooms. The largest holds 100 and includes two grand pianos. In addition an open access library and art room are available for Guests' use. The day begins and ends with a period of worship that is open to all who wish to attend.

The atmosphere is special and all who work here want guests to use this to enhance their own work and lives.

Event Types
Guided group retreats, guided individual retreats, own course programme, accredited courses.

Subject Specialities
Arts & crafts, self expression, inner process, meditation, prayer, health & healing, food & gardening, earth mysteries.

Eco-tourism features
Set in Birmingham's largest organically managed garden.

Other Places and Organisations

Atlow Mill Centre
Atlow Mill
Hognaston
Ashbourne
Derbyshire
DE6 1PX
Own Course Programme

Playroom at Canon Frome
Canon Frome
Ledbury
Herefordshire
HR8 2TD
Venue for Hire

Darby House
10 The Grove
Southey Street
Nottingham
NG7 4BQ
Bed & Breakfast

Edward King House
The Old Palace
Minster Yard
Lincoln
LN2 1PU
Bed & Breakfast
℡ 01522 528778

The Eirene Centre
The Old School
Clopton
Kettering
Northamptonshire
NN14 3DZ
Venue for Hire

Hoar Cross Hall
Hoar Cross
Lichfield
Staffordshire
DE13 8QS
Retreat House

Holycombe
Whichford
Shipston-on-Stour
Warwickshire
CV36 5PH
Own Course Programme

Other Places and Organisations

Igloo Backpackers Hostel
110 Mansfield Road
Nottingham
NG1 3HL
Bed & Breakfast

Launde Abbey
East Norton
Leicester
LE7 9XB
Retreat House

Morley Retreat & Conference House
Rose Cottage
Church Lane
Morley
Ilkeston
Derbyshire
DE7 6DE
Retreat House

Oak Barn Workshops
Nordybank Nurseries
Clee St Margaret
Craven Arms
Shropshire
SY7 9DT
Venue for Hire

Offa House
Offchurch
Leamington Spa
Warwickshire
CV33 9AS
Retreat House
✆ 01926 423309

Parkdale Yoga Centre
10 Parkdale West
Wolverhampton
West Midlands
WV1 4TE
Retreat House

The Practice
The Manor House
Kings Norton
Leicester
LE7 9BA
Retreat House
✆ 0116 259 9211

Tara Centre
Ashe Hall
Ash Lane
Etwall
Derby
DE65 6HT
Own Course Programme

Wales

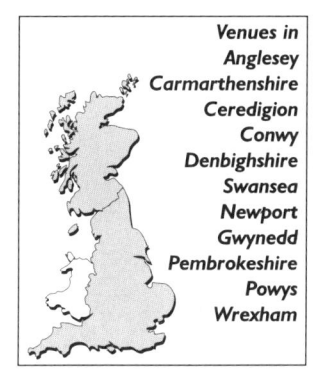

Venues in
Anglesey
Carmarthenshire
Ceredigion
Conwy
Denbighshire
Swansea
Newport
Gwynedd
Pembrokeshire
Powys
Wrexham

Outdoor Alternative 63
Anglesey Healing 49
Life Foundation 56
Trigonos 61
Bryn Awel 62
Snowdon Lodge 63
Coleg y Groes 62
Westward Lodges 64
Vajraloka 64
Ancient Healing 48
Hafod 62
Penybryn 63
Taraloka 64
Gwalia 62
Rainbow Rose 59
Spirit Horse 60
ABERYSTWYTH
Woodlands 55
Old Rectory 57
Cryndir 52 ◆ **Cwmllechwedd Fawr 53**
Cwrt Y Cylchau 62
Pen Rhiw 58
Mandala 63
Nolton Cottage 63
Trericket Mill 64
Plas Taliaris 63
Coleg Trefeca 51
Heartspring 54
Buckland Hall 50
Glorious Wales 62
West Usk Lighthouse 64
CARDIFF

Places to BE

Places to BE 2003/Page 47

Ancient Healing Ways

🟊 http://www.ancienthealingways.co.uk

Philippa Bondy
Parc Bothy
Tan-y-bwlch
Maentwrog
Blaenau Ffestiniog
Gwynedd
LL41 3AQ

☏ 01766 590685
✉ info@ancienthealingways.co.uk

✔ **Retreat House**
✔ **Own Course Programme**

In the timeless open space of Snowdonia's mystical mountains, Ancient Healing Ways invites you to explore, experience and 'just be' deeper inside yourself and the magic of the natural world.
Our courses are nature-based spiritual practices rooted in indigenous and shamanic traditions. If you are one who dares to look inside your being; one who wishes to cross the shore to arrive more fully into the 'present' and come closer to your true nature, we offer you initiatory courses including Vision Fast and Ancient Council. We touch your primal essence from the wild and edge-y to the eternal nature of a flower or a mountain. Supported with safety and kindness, we carry these old ways to open hearts and honour our beloved earth.

We are situated in the most beautiful setting – a forest of ancient oak trees resting in wild landscape.
Our base is an old cottage which has been tastefully renovated with wind and solar power. If you wish to camp, the rugged and varied landscape provides open spaces or secret hideaways.

Places to BE 2004/Page 48

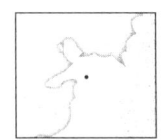

Wales/Gwynedd

Anglesey Healing Centre

🌟 http://www.angleseyhealingcentre.co.uk

The Anglesey Healing Centre is situated on the beautiful island of Anglesey between the mountains of Snowdonia and the Irish Sea. We are convenient for the high-speed ferry to Ireland. Close to several beaches, this is a wonderful place to walk, relax, and unwind. The island is rich in sacred sites; burial chambers and standing stones. A small family run centre, we welcome people seeking peace and quiet and an opportunity to go inward, in a healing and spiritual environment. We offer a self-contained, purpose-built space for personal retreats. Designed for one or two people, we can accommodate most dietary requirements and the retreat includes all meals and a healing treatment of your choice each day. We run group retreats on bank holiday weekends, "A Course in Miracles" Retreats and Reiki 1 and 2 classes. We have an extensive library of New Age books and tapes which guests are welcome to browse, and a beautiful, secluded garden for their pleasure. Retreats and courses are facilitated by Vivien Candlish, a Reiki Master since 1992, and "A Course in Miracles" teacher for eight years. The Centre is warm and comfortable with a welcoming and informal atmosphere.

Event Types
Retreat weekends, Personal retreats, Reiki 1 and 2 classes, "A Course In Miracles" Retreats, Guided visits to Sacred Sites.

Subject Specialities
Healing, Personal Growth, Spirituality, Meditation.

Suitability or Specialism
Adults

Vivien Candlish
Bro Dawel, Llangoed
Beaumaris
Anglesey
LL58 8PB
✆ 01248 490814
📠 01248 490195
✉ vivreiki@hotmail.com

✔ **Retreat House**
✔ **Own Course Programme**

🛏 Centre: 6 bedspaces. (2 singles, 2 doubles.) 2 shared bathrooms. Self-contained Personal Retreat Space: double with bathroom.

🍽 We cater for vegetarians, vegans and meat-eaters. Some of the vegetables are from our organic vegetable garden.

🚌 Train or coach to Bangor (North Wales), N57 bus to Glanrafon, or taxi

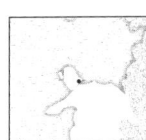

Wales/Anglesey

Buckland Hall

http://www.bucklandhall.co.uk

Martin Fleming
Buckland Hall
Bwlch
Brecon
Powys
LD3 7JJ

✆ 01874 730276
📠 01874 730740
✉ info@bucklandhall.co.uk

✓ **Retreat House**
✓ **Venue for hire**
🛏 68 bedspaces (4 singles, 20 twins, 2 doubles, 5 family rooms.)
🍽 Exclusively vegetarian, special diets.
♿ Wheelchair access.
Focus Open

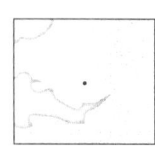

Buckland Hall is an amazing space that you can make your own. It is a dedicated venue for all types of group events - whether they be celebrations, courses, retreats and get-togethers. Groups with exclusive use feel they own the place. You have privacy, focus and the opportunity to create the right experience for your session. Buckland Hall is set in 60 acres of gardens and parkland amidst the spectacular Brecon Beacons and overlooking the River Usk. It offers 68 bed spaces in 31 excellent en-suite bedrooms. However, since the activity spaces can handle up to 130, many groups use additional local accommodation. Catering is exclusively vegetarian, gourmet standard and served in style. Special diets are catered for and groups determine the style of menu and schedule of mealtimes. Self-catering is a possibility for trusted groups. Access and special bedrooms for disabled needs. Facilities include: large meeting rooms; meditation room; treatment rooms; snooker and recreation rooms. Buckland Hall can host all types of personal growth courses, celebrations, get-togethers, conferences. Detoxification and therapy sessions. Alternative weddings (registered venue) and celebrations.

Event Types
Guided group retreats, business retreats.
Subject Specialities
Personal growth, group process, meditation, celebrations, inner process, health & healing, earth mysteries, self expression, body & breathwork, alternative lifestyles & technology, arts & crafts, counselling, ritual & shamanic.
Suitability or Specialism
Adults(++), couples(++), families with children, women, men, older people.

Coleg Trefeca

http://www.trefeca.org.uk

In the heart of the Brecon Beacons National Park, Coleg Trefeca is a centre for conferences, retreats and lay training. The historic birthplace of Howell Harris, leader of the Methodist Revival in Wales in the 18th century, it is now a listed building, set in 5 acres of grounds. Harris established here a remarkable Christian "family", Teulu Trefeca, which was a virtually self-sufficient community, representing more than 70 different trades and crafts. The College houses a museum including artefacts from the time of Howell Harris. Today the sense of Christian family is still strong. The atmosphere of the house and grounds make this an excellent place to relax, away from day-to-day pressures. Individuals may book into our own course programme, which includes day and residential courses and designated holiday weeks. Please contact us for further details. Groups are welcome to book the centre when available, for their own events.

Event Types
Guided group retreats, own course programme.

Subject Specialities
Prayer, arts & crafts, self expression.

Suitability or Specialism
Adults(++), couples, families with children, older people.

Focus
Christian

Gethin Rhys
Coleg Trefeca, College Lane
Trefeca, Brecon
Powys
LD3 0PP

☎ 01874 711423
📠 01874 712212
✉ post@trefeca.org.uk
✓ **Bed & Breakfast**
✓ **Own Course Programme**
✓ **Venue for hire**

🛏 39 bedspaces (18 twins, 1 family room.)
🍽 Special diets.
♿ Wheelchair access.
🚆 Lifts available from Abergavenny (18 miles). A few buses to Talgarth but public transport very limited.

Wales/Powys

Cryndir

http://www.cryndir.co.uk

Anita Lear
Cryndir
Nantmel
Llandrindod Wells
Powys
LD1 6EH

✆ 01597 825505
📠 01597 824484
✉ lear@marquetry.co.uk

✔ **Retreat House**
✔ **Venue for hire**

↝ 16 bedspaces (3 doubles, 7 futons and 6 mattresses in workshop areas)
🚆 Train to Llandrindod Wells

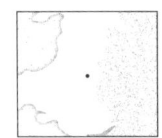

Incredibly beautiful all year round retreat let for hire with a complete difference: unusual 16th century oak beamed Quaker meeting house. Can be used as either holiday let or as holistic workshop hire space for meditation, yoga, drumming, chanting, etc. Well suited to groups or friends sharing the bedrooms and workrooms as a bunkhouse, who are willing to muck in, run around naked, meditate, have a holiday or just camp if they wish. Have a quiet break or bring a group and run workshops. The Cryndir is set in 2 wooded acres, 4 fields from nearest house, surrounded by woodlands and rural Welsh hills. It is very secluded. Also very suitable for walkers and birdwatchers and other groups etc who want peace and quiet.

For workshops food can also be cooked and supplied or just look after yourselves. Bookable for days, weekends and weeks. Camp too, from sweat lodges and bonfires or fun in sauna (fits 9 people). Available all year round with large log fire, central and under-floor heating. See website for prices or email enquiry. 7 miles from Ellan valley reservoirs and 5 miles from Llandrindod. Map reference: 267223 304941

Event Types
Self directed retreats, business retreats, working holidays, family groups.

Suitability or Specialism
Everyone welcome.

Cwmllechwedd Fawr

http://www.cwmllechwedd.u-net.com

Cwmllechwedd Fawr is a working hill farm of just over one hundred acres nestling in the Radnorshire hills in the ancient Welsh Cantriff of Maelienydd. It is set back a quarter of a mile from the road and overlooks a wide valley through which the Camdwr flows. The borderlands of Wales – the Marches – are rich in history. Within easy striking distance are Iron-Age forts, evidence of Roman occupation and splendid sections of Offa's Dyke. Places well worth a visit include Powis Castle with its terraced gardens, homely Stokesay Castle, small towns like Montgomery and Presteigne and the Marcher towns Shrewsbury, Ludlow and Hereford. On the Welsh side is the Edwardian spa town Llandrindod Wells, pretty Llanidloes, Rhayader with the great Elan Valley dams, and the wild and beautiful Cambrian Mountains which sweep westwards towards the sea. There are several small and interesting art galleries in the area, too.

Cwmllechwedd Fawr offers two centrally heated double bedrooms each with its own spacious adjoining bathroom. Breakfast is served in the large farm kitchen, where all cooking is done in the Aga. After a day's excursion supper is served in the elegant dining room with its stone floor and large wood-burning stove.

As a 'working' farm with sheep dogs and several cats, Cwmllechwedd is not a suitable place for small children or pets, although we do make exceptions! Smoking is an 'outdoor' activity here.

Where possible and according to the season we serve our own organically grown vegetables, salads, fruit and home-produced meat.

Please bring your own alcohol as we do not have a licence.

Eco-tourism features
Organic farm committed to conservation in an area of tranquility.

John Underwood
Cwmllechwedd Fawr
Llanbister
Llandrindod Wells
Powys
LD1 6UH

✆ 01597 840267
✆ 01597 840267
✉ postmaster@cwmllechwedd.u-net.com

✔ **Bed & Breakfast**

🛏 2 double rooms. £30 single, £25 shared.
🍽 Special diets catered for.

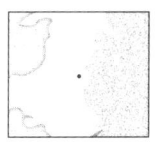

Heartspring

http://www.heartspring.co.uk

Madeline Lynfield
Hill House
Llansteffan
Carmarthen
SA33 5JG
✆ 01267 241999
✉ info@heartspring.co.uk
✔ **Retreat House**
✔ **Bed & Breakfast**
⌁ 9 bedspaces (1 single, 1 twin, 2 double / family rooms.)
🍽 Exclusively vegetarian, special diets. B&B and half board.
♿ No wheelchair access.
🚌 Bus from Carmarthen to Llansteffan, Sticks Hotel. Steep driveway is after the 4th house beyond the hotel, opposite the church.

Focus Open to all

Heartspring is surrounded by stunning coastal scenery yet in an easily accessible part of South West Wales. Our grand Victorian house is superbly sited on a hill overlooking a designated Coastal Conservation Area with magnificent views of the beaches, the Norman castle and sleepy untouched village.

What we offer
We offer a tranquil and enriching environment for a relaxing holiday or for Individual retreats and mini-breaks. These can be tailor made to your requirements with the optional addition of complementary therapy and teaching sessions such as Massage, Healing, Profound Relaxation, Meditation and many others from local practitioners.

The house
Heartspring has been lovingly restored with an emphasis on the use of toxic-free environmentally-friendly materials and the rooms are all decorated with natural paints and varnishes. We also have lovely pure spring water for bathing and drinking, and solar heating panels for hot water. All our meals are fully organic and vegetarian and we offer a full equipped vegetarian kitchen for those wanting to self-cater.

The house is south facing with large windows to drink in the stunning scenery, and we offer a very peaceful and tranquil atmosphere, free of television and other associated noises.

We have an inspiring environment to help those looking to find their own inner healing, peace and vitality and to let their spirits fly.

Eco-tourism features
Heartspring has been completely renovated using environment-friendly toxic-free materials and paints. We also have solar panels, spring water and serve only organic vegetarian food.

Inspiring Breaks - Woodlands

Whether you're looking for inspiration, a healing retreat, or to (re)discover your direction and purpose, here is the near-perfect setting. With panoramic and utterly serene views over thickly wooded valleys and rolling green hills, the house is set in a huge, totally secluded garden and natural woodland, with its own babbling stream and waterfalls feeding four delightful pools. If you spend some time working in the garden or on permaculture design, you could even stay here free! There is a unique library of books on personal and spiritual development, including 35 on the subject of discovering your purpose, vocation and ideal work ... and making a happy living from it! Looking out from the picture window, which captures the morning sun, the sky is decorated with the aerial acrobatics of swallows and hawks, and at the end of a one-mile no-through-road, birdsong is virtually all you will hear! There is a large bathroom with shower and bath and the sitting room contains a very fully equipped kitchenette, spacious writing bureau, and even a Hi-Fi system. The TV may be better used to watch video recordings from a library of hundreds of documentaries, films and comedy/satire programmes. Organic food can be delivered. Within the sheltered 2-acre garden, there are many totally secluded places and a choice of outdoor seats including a hammock. A swinging bench is positioned for the perfect view and the best of the sun, with patio heater for evening stargazing.

Event Types
Self directed retreats.
Subject Specialities
Finding your vocation, personal and spiritual development library, meditation, organic food & gardening, conservation work, outdoor activities & sport, health & healing.
Suitability or Specialism
Adults, couples, older people.
Eco-tourism features
Fresh air heating (heat pump) in use.

Alan Selkirk
Woodlands
Banhadlog
Llanidloes
Powys
SY18 6JR

℡ 0870 207 0870
✆ 0870 208 0870
✉ aselkirk@smartsolutions.org.uk

✔ **Retreat House**
✔ **Bed & Breakfast**
⇨ 2 bedspaces (2 doubles.) Mainly individual self catering. Individual B&B (£24 to £29 single, £19 to £24 shared), no smoking in buildings.

🚌 Collection service from local station

Wales/Powys

Life Foundation - Dru Yoga Centre

http://www.lifefoundation.org.uk

Cherry Knight
Life Foundation
Nant Ffrancon
Bethesda
Bangor
Gwynedd
LL57 3LX

☏ 01248 602900
✆ 01248 602004
✉ enquiries@lifefoundation.org.uk

✓ **Own Course Programme**

- 3 singles, 20 twins.
- Exclusively vegetarian.

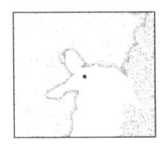

The Life Foundation International Course Centre is situated in the beautiful Welsh Mountains of the Snowdonia National Park, North Wales. It is the home of The World Peace Flame, a world-wide peace initiative where seven living flames were lit in July 1999 by peacemakers in Africa, Australia, Europe, Asia, the Middle East and North America and united to create "The World Peace Flame". For details on this project please contact us.

The Life Foundation is a committed team of individuals from a wide range of backgrounds providing spiritual awareness, self-empowerment, and self-development courses. We teach techniques that integrate the body-heart and mind, creating physical well-being and emotional balance that enables the individual to access their highest potential. We specialise in Dru Yoga, Meditation Retreats and Spiritual Development Courses. We also take our work into areas of conflict, war zones and decision making arenas throughout the world.
"Transform the world by giving people the tools to transform themselves."

Event Types
Own course programme, teacher training.

Subject Specialities
Health & yoga, spiritual self development.

Suitability or Specialism
Adults.

The Old Rectory and Retreat Cottage

http://www.go-wales.org

In the heart of the Pembrokeshire National Park in South Wales you find this extraordinary place. Here you can relax and heal your soul, body and spirit.

Two beautifully renovated C18th listed homes have their own charm and outstanding views over Newport Bay. From the slopes of Carn Ingli (angel mountain) the panoramic view extends along the famous coastline, beach, estuary, up to rocky crags and open moorlands.

Set in the acre of walled garden with separate private and communal areas, this historic site offers a thoughtfully designed venue for all interests. Here you can cook, dine, play, sunbathe, hide or pick our ripening fruits. Quietly situated 300m from the road it is surrounded by meadows.

Newport (Trefdraeth) is only a mile away. This ancient market town has a Norman castle, several excellent pubs and restaurants for all tastes and a wholefood store. Explore Newport's galleries, craft workshops, the golf course, the boat club and its one mile long beach.

A short walk takes you to the remarkable 186 mile long Pembrokeshire coast path, to dolmens, historic sites, wooded valleys and secluded coves. Nearby you find the Stonehenge Bluestone site in the Preseli mountains, an C11th Celtic cross, Neolithic tombs and stone circles.

Accommodation
Rectory has 6 bedrooms, Cottage has 3 bedrooms. Welsh Tourist Board 4 star accredited self-catering accommodation. Caterers available (from £10 per person per night). Large and smaller indoor spaces. One acre private walled garden. No smoking in buildings. Public transport available. Venue for hire for all ages, each property hired individually or together. Parties of 2-20 welcome.

Event Types
Venue suitable for self directed workshops and retreats. Family holidays. Reunions. Business workshops.

Subject Specialities
Previously used for meditation retreats, health and healing, storytelling, writing, martial arts, dance and musical workshops. Walking, cycling, rock climbing, astrology, Celtic culture, historic study, geological study and painting groups.

Carol Griffith
Gelli-Olau
Fishguard Road
Newport
Pembrokeshire
SA42 0UE
℡ 01239 820277
℡ 01239 820279
✉ go.wales@virgin.net

✓ **Retreat House**
✓ **Holiday Operator**
✓ **Venue for hire**
↪ 20 bedspaces (2 singles, 4 doubles, 1 twin, 2 family rooms, cots available).

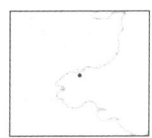

Wales/Pembrokeshire

Pen Rhiw

http://www.stdavids.co.uk/penrhiw

Tim Sime, Pen Rhiw, St Davids Haverfordwest SA62 6PG
© 01437 721821
✆ 01437 721821
✉ penrhiw@stdavids.co.uk
- ✓ **Retreat House**
- ✓ **Own Course Programme**
- ✓ **Venue for hire**

group full board (£43), large indoor & several small spaces

🚃 21 bedrms: up to 35 places; almost all with washbasins. 4 doubles (1 en-suite), 7 singles, 7 twins, 1 family. Other beds/spaces available. Full board, B&B, self-catering, central heating, no smoking in buildings, meditation room.
🍽 Special diets.
♿ Wheelchair access.
🚆 Train or coach to Haverfordwest, then taxi or bus to St Davids.

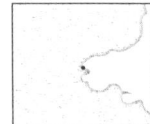

Focus
Meditation

In the beautiful, powerful setting of the St Davids Peninsula in Britain's only coastal national park, Pen Rhiw is a fine, early Victorian rectory with a welcoming atmosphere. The main group room, a converted chapel with wonderful acoustics, is 52ft x 17ft. There is a living room with a log fire, over an acre of secluded grounds, a woodland terraced garden and seven acres of wildflower hay meadow which include rare species. It's a ten minute peaceful walk to the medieval Cathedral and Close and Whitesands Bay is a mile away. There is excellent, plentiful homecooked vegetarian food (organic garden). Open to all, families with children welcome.

Specialities include meditation workshops, guided walks (including ancient sites). Leader led spiritual groups, creative and performance arts, yoga, t'ai-chi, psychology, astrology, walkers.

The Living Guru, Swami Shree Shivkrupanandji, has Pen Rhiw as his UK base for Samarpan Meditation workshops. This pure form of meditation connects people, simply, with Universal Consciousness.

http://www.counserve.co.uk/rainbowrosecircl

Rainbow Rose Retreats

ESOTERIC GARDENING: In a secluded 8-acres of oak-woods the old farmhouse offers a basic homely welcome, (electric heating in all rooms, plus log fires in parlour and dining room). While much potential for enhancing comfort and creating gardens awaits future realisation, we are offering a space in the "wild-wood" for guided retreats and relaxing themed holiday-workshops. Book the whole venue for your own self-catering holidays. We also offer working holidays for the more energetic! Within 8 miles of the extensive sandy beach at Aberdovey, and of the Centre for Alternative Technology at Pantperthog, day-trips are possible. Our emphasis is upon healing being a gentle unfolding into soul-potential, viewing disease and distress as gateways into the next stage of unfoldment. Available, at your choice, are client-centred counselling sessions, Bach Flower Remedies, Radionics Treatment, Dream-work, White Eagle Healing; and for groups, the Talking/Listening-Stick or Conch.

Event Types
Guided group retreats, guided individual retreats, self directed retreats, own course programme, working holidays.

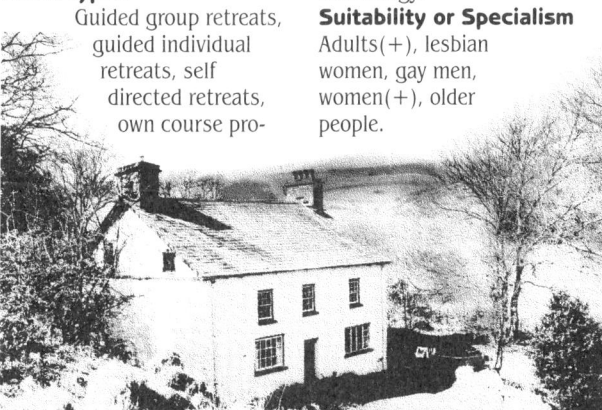

Subject Specialities
Esoteric gardening, meditation, group process, inner process, ritual & shamanic, counselling, food & gardening, health & healing, self expression, conservation work, prayer, alternative lifestyles & technology.

Suitability or Specialism
Adults(+), lesbian women, gay men, women(+), older people.

Jane W Trevelyan
and Elyan P Stephens
Cefnllecoediog
Happy Valley
Pennal
Machynlleth, Powys
SY20 9LE

☏ 01654 791319
✆ 01654 767575
✉ stelyan@onetel.net.uk
✔ **Retreat House**
✔ **Own Course Programme**
✔ **Venue for hire**
⚐ 10 bedspaces (1 double, 4 family rooms).
🍽 Exclusively vegetarian.
🚃 Train to Machynlleth then Bus 29 to Cwrt and 20 minute walk ... or else train to Tywyn and be met by us (minibus)

Focus Ancient Wisdom and New Age Christian

Wales/Powys

Spirit Horse Camps

http://www.spirithorse.co.uk

Erika Indra
19 Holmwood Gardens
London
N3 3NS

✆ 020 8346 3660
✉ indraerika@hotmail.com
✔ **Retreat House**
✔ **Own Course Programme**
✔ **Venue for hire**
group full board (£17 to £25),
group self catering (£6-£12)

⌁ Space/quarters for 10 to 200 in Celtic roundhouses, yurts, tipis, bedouin tents. Huge 38ft Celtic roundhouse. Viking mead hall-style kitchen seating 150. Many other spaces.
🍽 Special diets.
♿ None (wildland).

🚐 We collect from Machynlleth Railway Station

Spirit Horse - founded and directed by Shivam O'Brien, Irish ceremonialist and storyteller, and Erika Indra, Hungarian healer, psychic and counsellor - has for 13 years offered a wide range of its own camps as well as hosting other organisations. Set amidst 2000 acres of unspoilt Wales among waterfalls, rockpools, woods and mountains, we offer a unique and unforgettable experience.

Focus Ancient wisdom traditions: shamanic, Celtic, Buddhist, Sufi, Native American, Eastern, enlightenment traditions etc ... looking for the common thread.

Course Programme
Our courses and workshops spearhead our research into and rediscovery of ritual, traditional story and ancient wisdom ways, providing balance and refuge for individuals living in a modern world heedless of such older, more rooted and sustainable values. Our personal and ceremonial transformations include:
• Sacred Man, Sacred Woman (4-day ritual intensive to heal and renew relations between men and women)
• Messages of Beauty (5-day life-changing ceremonial intensive)
• Enlightenment Intensive (for deep spiritual inquiry)
• Ongoing Men's, Women's and Young Women's Lodge programmes.
• A ceremonial Children's Camp for 8-17 year olds
• Festivals of performing arts in May and August for all the family, recreating sacred community
Contact us for a full brochure.
Venue Hire
Our summer village is the main British venue for large shamanic, ritual and earth-loving conferences and workshops. We have also catered for large Buddhist groups and retreats. Other organisations that use or have used our venue include Leo Rutherford and Eagle's Wing, HH Chhimed Rigdzin Rinpoche, Victor Sanchez, Ngak'chang Rinpoche, Shenpen Lama and the Awakened Heart Sangha ...
Eco-tourism features
Reforestation project. "Sacred Ecology" youth training programme. Rare wildlife/habitats. Low-impact, community-built mythical and sacred architecture. "Deep ecology" realised in traditional indigenous ritual space. Exemplary recycling. Compost toilets. No electricity.

Trigonos

🕸 http://www.trigonos.org

Trigonos lies within the Snowdonia National Park on the edge of the village of Nantlle. It is a site of spectacular natural beauty by the side of Llyn (Lake) Nantlle with a direct view across the lake and up the valley to Snowdon. The grounds include herb and vegetable gardens, fields, coppices, a stream and access to the lake itself. There is space for walking and quiet reflection, and easy access to the local countryside.

Venue Hire
Facilities include: gallery, suitable for yoga, tai chi, movement, performances; large meeting room (up to 30 people); small meeting room, art studio/study centre, lounge, library and 16 bedrooms.
We host groups running their own education and training programmes, retreats, holidays, art workshops, etc.

Course Programme
Our own courses include weaving and dyeing, art, social action and development, health & wellbeing and family-based events.

Bed & Breakfast
We welcome visitors of all ages, B&B or full-board (subject to availability).

Food
Delicious home-cooked meals largely, but not exclusively, vegetarian; increasing use of organic and home grown produce. Special diets can be catered for.

Frances Smith
Trigonos, Plas Baladeulyn
Nantlle, Caernarfon LL54 6BW
✆ 01286 882388
📠 01286 882424
✉ info@trigonos.org

✔ **Retreat House**
✔ **Bed & Breakfast**
✔ **Own Course Programme**
✔ **Venue for hire**
group full board (£26 to £43), large indoor space & more

🛏 25 in mostly en-suite rooms, can be increased to 35. No smoking indoors.
♿ Wheelchair access to public spaces, some bedrooms.
🚌 Bangor Station then Bus 5 to Nantlle or Caernarfon. Bus 80 from Caernarfon to Nantlle, stops outside Trigonos.

Focus Interfaith

Other Places and Organisations

Bryn Awel
Llangwm
Corwen
Denbighshire
LL21 0RB
Bed & Breakfast

Coleg y Groes
Corwen
Denbighshire
LL21 0AU
Retreat House

Cwrt Y Cylchau
Llanfair Clydogau
Lampeter
Ceredigion
SA48 8LJ
Retreat House
℡ 01570 493526

Glorious Wales
35 Owensfield
Caswell
Swansea
SA3 4LA
℡ 020 7278 0297
Self-Catering

Gwalia Farm
Cemmaes
Machynlleth
Powys
SY20 9PZ
Bed & Breakfast

Hafod Cottage & Art Studio
Hafod
Maentwrog
Blaenau Ffestiniog
Gwynedd
LL41 3AQ
Self-Catering

Other Places and Organisations

Mandala Yoga Ashram
Pantypistyll
Llansadwrn
Llandeilo
Carmarthenshire
SA19 8NR
Own Course Programme

Nolton Cottage
Nolton Haven
Haverfordwest
Pembrokeshire
SA62 3NW
Self-Catering

Outdoor Alternative
Cerrig yr Adar
Rhoscolyn
Holyhead
Anglesey
LL65 2NQ
Holiday Operator

Penybryn
Rhyd
Penrhyndeudraeth
LL48 6ST
Own Course Programme

Snowdon Lodge
Lawrence House
Church Street
Tremadog
Portmadog
Gwynedd
LL49 9PS
Bed & Breakfast

Plas Taliaris
Llandeilo
Carmarthenshire
SA19 7NL
Venue for Hire

Other Places and Organisations

Trericket Mill
Erwood
Builth Wells
Powys
LD2 3TQ
Bed & Breakfast

The West Usk Lighthouse
St Brides Wentlooge
Newport
Gwent
NP10 8SF
Bed & Breakfast

Westward Lodges
Cwr-coed
Y Ffôr
Pwllheli
Gwynedd
LL53 6YA
Venue for Hire

Taraloka Buddhist Retreat Centre for Women
Bettisfield
Whitchurch
Shropshire
SY13 2LD
Own Course Programme
℅ 01948 710646

Vajraloka Buddhist Meditation Centre for Men
Tyn-y-Ddol
Treddol
Corwen
Denbighshire
LL21 0EN
Retreat House

South West England

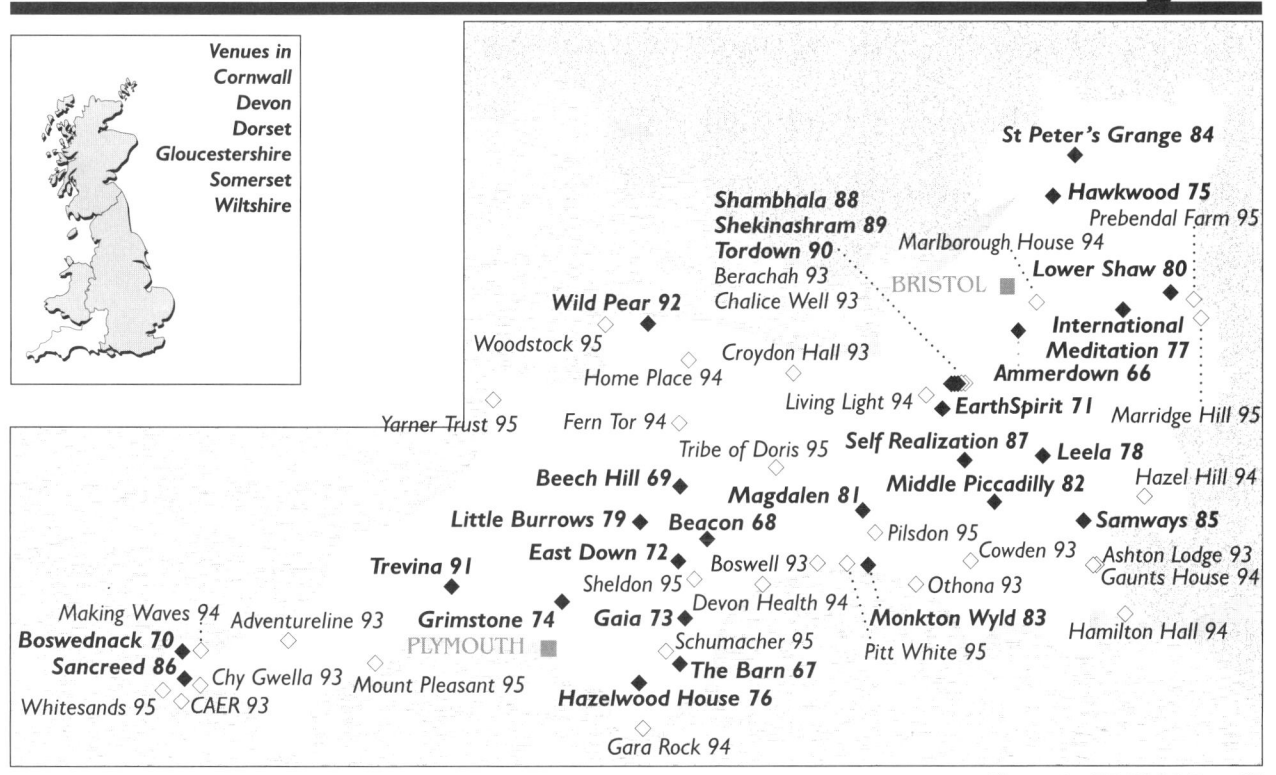

Venues in
Cornwall
Devon
Dorset
Gloucestershire
Somerset
Wiltshire

St Peter's Grange 84
Hawkwood 75
Prebendal Farm 95
Shambhala 88
Shekinashram 89
Tordown 90
Marlborough House 94
Berachah 93
BRISTOL
Lower Shaw 80
Wild Pear 92
Chalice Well 93
International
Meditation 77
Woodstock 95
Croydon Hall 93
Ammerdown 66
Home Place 94
Yarner Trust 95
Fern Tor 94
Living Light 94
EarthSpirit 71
Marridge Hill 95
Tribe of Doris 95
Self Realization 87
Leela 78
Beech Hill 69
Middle Piccadilly 82
Hazel Hill 94
Little Burrows 79
Magdalen 81
Samways 85
Beacon 68
Pilsdon 95
Trevina 91
East Down 72
Cowden 93
Ashton Lodge 93
Boswell 93
Othona 93
Gaunts House 94
Sheldon 95
Making Waves 94
Adventureline 93
Grimstone 74
Gaia 73
Devon Health 94
Monkton Wyld 83
Boswednack 70
PLYMOUTH
Schumacher 95
Hamilton Hall 94
Sancreed 86
Chy Gwella 93
Mount Pleasant 95
The Barn 67
Pitt White 95
Whitesands 95
CAER 93
Hazelwood House 76
Gara Rock 94

Places to BE 2004/Page 65

The Ammerdown Centre

🕸 http://www.ammerdown.org

Judith Raby
Ammerdown Centre, Radstock
Somerset, BA3 5SW
© 01761 433709
✆ 01761 433094
✉ centre@ammerdown.org
✔ **Retreat House**
✔ **Bed & Breakfast**
✔ **Own Course Programme**
✔ **Venue for hire**

group full board (£36 to £50.50), large indoor space, several small spaces

🛏 58 bedspaces (31 singles, 7 twins, 1 double, 3 family rooms).
🍴 Special diets.
♿ Wheelchair access.
🚆 Bath Spa station then regular bus services to Radstock, then taxi to Centre.

Focus Christian and Interfaith

Ammerdown is a retreat and conference centre located in beautiful, tranquil Somerset countryside. It has an excellent reputation for good food and a friendly atmosphere that sets the scene for an enjoyable experience.

Our programme includes spirituality retreats, interfaith, justice and peace, painting, holidays (literature, crafts, over 50s), prayer weekends, circle dance and day courses. There are our 'Quiet Spaces', including self-catering facilities, for those who wish to come and be away from the telephone and day to day pressures to walk, read, be listened to, or simply 'be'.

The Centre also provides excellent day or residential facilities for groups wishing to organise their own retreats, conferences and training, free from the many interruptions of the workplace.

As a holiday base there are many places of interest in the locality such as Wells, Bath, Glastonbury, Longleat and Cheddar.

Event Types
Guided group retreats, guided individual retreats, self directed retreats, own course programme, accredited courses.

Subject Specialities
Prayer, meditation, arts & crafts.

Suitability or Specialism
Adults, couples, families with children, women, men, young people 12 to 17, children under 12, older people.

🔗 http://www.sharpham-trust.org/barn.htm

The Barn Rural Retreat

Half-hidden behind giant beech trees on a hillside overlooking the river Dart, the Barn is one of the best-kept secrets in the English retreat circuit. Peace and quiet, wonderful organic food, and the healing effect of meditation and reflection in a stunning natural location are some of the reasons people return again and again to take time out there from their usual routine. The Barn was established 16 years ago to provide an environment where people could spend anything from one week to six months practising meditation and learning to integrate it into their day-to-day lives. Supported by two residential managers, a changing group of up to eight retreatants share the gardening, cooking and household tasks, as well as three periods a day of silent group meditation. Although Buddhist inspired, all faiths (or none) are equally welcome at the Barn. No meditation experience is needed, just willingness to participate. Simple instructions are given if required, and teachers visit twice a week to answer questions. In term time there is the opportunity to attend evening talks at nearby Sharpham College.

During the afternoons and evenings, retreatants are encouraged to explore the 600-acre Sharpham estate of which the Barn property is a part, or pursue their own practice and creative activities. There is an optional yoga lesson once a week.

Block booking is possible in the quiet season, when, in consultation with the managers, a group may wish to create its own programme, whilst making full use of the Barn facilities.

Eco-tourism features
All organic cuisine, work period mainly in organic gardens.

Sally McCarter
The Barn
Lower Sharpham Barton
Ashprington
Totnes, Devon
TQ9 7DX
✆ 01803 732661
✆ 01803 732718
✉ barn@sharphamcollege.org
✔ Retreat House
✔ Own Course Programme
✔ Venue for hire
group full board (£11 to £17), large indoor space, several small spaces
🛏 9 bedspaces (7 singles, 1 twin).
🍽 Exclusively vegetarian, special diets.
♿ None alas.
🚆 Train or coach to Totnes then 10 minute taxi ride.
Focus Eclectic but Buddhist inspired.

South West England/Devon

The Beacon Centre

🌐 http://www.beacon-centre.com

Ceri Fitz-Gerald
Cutteridge Farm
Whitestone, Exeter
EX4 2HE
✆ 01392 811203
📠 01392 811203
✉ ceri@beacon-centre.com
✔ **Retreat House**
✔ **Bed & Breakfast**
✔ **Own Course Programme**
✔ **Venue for hire**
group full board (£35), large indoor & several small spaces
🛏 24 bedspaces (6 twin, 2x3 bed, 1x4 bed, 1 double/twin). Individual/group self-catering, group full board, camping (10). B&B £18.
🍽 Exclusively vegetarian/organic (subject to availability), special diets.
🚌 Three and a half miles from both the train and coach station in Exeter.

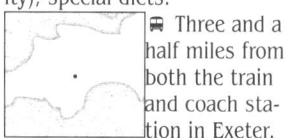

The Beacon Centre is situated within the attractive Devon hills. We offer a warm and welcoming venue for groups who are seeking a supportive, family atmosphere within which to work and be. Self-catering groups can enjoy uninterrupted use of the centre, including our well equipped and spacious kitchen.

Fine, varied and wholesome vegetarian food is our speciality for which we endeavour to use organic ingredients wherever possible.

The centre is cared for by a developing community of families and individuals who live at the farm. Our ethos is one of grounded, co-operative living, that seeks to restore harmony within ourselves, each other and the planet.

The centre is open all year round, it is regularly used for courses in bodywork, professional training, therapeutic workshops, dance, movement and creative expression. We also work in association with a number of other organisations, providing day and residential space, for work with children and young people. For further information, please write or telephone.

http://web.onetel.net.uk/~beechhill

Beech Hill Community

Beech Hill is set in seven acres of grounds and gardens in a quiet, rural location midway between Dartmoor and Exmoor. Our course centre offers heated, small-dormitory accommodation; plus kitchen and large workspace suitable for t'ai chi, drumming, dance etc. The room is light and airy with a wood-burning stove, and opens on to a large lawn and gardens. A shady paddock provides good camping space, compost loo and outdoor shower. We offer superb wholefood catering using our own organic fruit and vegetables if available or, alternatively, courses can be self-catered. An outdoor swimming pool is available in summer months.

Event Types
Business retreats, accredited courses, working holidays.

Subject Specialities
Alternative lifestyles & technology, food & gardening, conservation work, rural skills, self expression, body & breathwork, health & healing, outdoor activities & sport, group process, ritual & shamanic.

Eco-tourism features
Communal living, organic growing, animals, compost toilet, reed bed system, recycling, cob building, site for local compost scheme.

Hazel or Sue
Beech Hill
Morchard Bishop
Crediton
Devon
EX17 6RF

✆ 01363 877228
✆ 01363 877587
✉ beechhill@ukonline.co.uk

✔ **Bed & Breakfast**
✔ **Venue for hire**
group full board (up to £32), large indoor space

⛉ 15 bedspaces (1 twin, 1 double, 2 dormitories).
🍽 Special diets.
♿ Limited wheelchair access.
🚂 Nearest railway station, Morchard Road, is 4 miles away. Bus from Exeter 3 times daily to Morchard Bishop (1 mile).

South West England/Devon

Boswednack Manor

Liz Gynn
Boswednack Manor
Zennor
St Ives
Cornwall
TR26 3DD

✆ 01736 794183
✔ **Retreat House**
✔ **Bed & Breakfast**
✔ **Own Course Programme**
✔ **Venue for hire**
group full board (£30 to £50), large indoor space
⌇ 10 bedspaces (1 single, 1 twin, 2 doubles, 1 family room).
🍽 Exclusively vegetarian, special diets.
🚆 Train to Penzance or St Ives then bus 8, 8a or 15 will stop at our gate.
Focus
Buddhist/Eco-spiritual

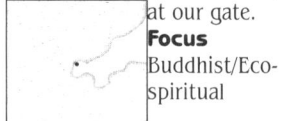

Boswednack Manor comprises an old granite farmhouse with a cottage and group of barns around a grassy courtyard. The house itself is run as vegetarian guesthouse, and "Campion Cottage" is let on a self-catering basis. The barn spaces include a 36 x 16ft group work room and a separate meditation room plus barns for chickens, goats etc! There is a large organic vegetable garden, beautiful ornamental gardens with pond, outside chessboard and two meadows. The house and garden look down to the sea which is a few minutes' walk away and the Penwith Moors – rich in ancient sites like Men-an-Tol – are adjacent too. We offer B&B, wildlife walks, self-guided and facilitated retreats. Our programme includes movement and meditation, Yoga, Native American and Shamanistic weeks, and Buddhist retreats. We welcome enquiries from those who wish to bring their own group (of up to 16) to this special centre.

Event Types
Guided group retreats, self directed retreats, own course programme.

Subject Specialities
Meditation, body & breathwork, earth mysteries, food & gardening, outdoor activities & sport.

Suitability or Specialism
Adults, couples, families with children.

Eco-tourism features
Solar water heating and organic garden.

EarthSpirit

Five miles from Glastonbury, EarthSpirit lies within the 'temenos' (sacred enclosure) of Avalon. Situated next to a wildlife reserve and a yew tree which is over 1,700 years old! EarthSpirit has a healing atmosphere but is not attached to any one tradition. We provide full facilities to groups of all kinds in our specially converted seventeenth century barn complex. The main hall is 52 feet long with oak timbers, reeds and stone walls. Mediaeval, but with modern comforts such as underfloor heating and a large wood stove. A high roof and skylights create a light, airy atmosphere. Neighbouring B&B and camping can boost numbers. Seven acres of fields and gardens. Druidic tree circle, therapy room, sweat lodge and hot tub all available. Phone for photos. £23/24 hours food/bed. Centre £130/day (Monday to Thursday), £150/day (Friday to Sunday).

Event Types
Guided group retreats, accredited courses, teacher training.

Subject Specialities
Health & healing.

Suitability or Specialism
Adults, couples.

David Taylor
EarthSpirit
Dundon
Somerton
TA11 6PE

© 01458 272161
℡ 01458 273796
✆ earth.spirit1@virgin.net

✔ **Retreat House**
✔ **Venue for hire**

⇨ 35 bedspaces (2 singles).
🍽 Exclusively vegetarian, special diets.
♿ Wheelchair access.

🚆 Castle Cary station 20 minutes by taxi (01963 351015)

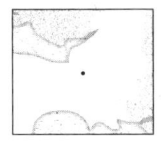

Focus Eco-spirituality

East Down Centre

Richard Jones
East Down Centre
Dunsford
Exeter
Devon
EX6 7AL

✆ 01647 24041
✉ richard@tia.co.uk

✔ **Venue for hire**

🛏 18 bedspaces.

Peaceful accommodation for small groups or workshops. No sharing with other groups. Self-catering or catered. Large group room. Sympathetically converted thatched barn set in beautiful country within the Dartmoor National Park.

http://www.gaiahouse.co.uk

Gaia House

Gaia House is set in the quiet and beautiful countryside of South Devon and the peace of the Retreat Centre provides a sanctuary of calm stillness.

We offer a full programme of group retreats throughout the year inspired by the Buddhist tradition. Each group retreat day includes a full schedule of sitting and walking meditation, group or individual interviews, a talk and meditation instructions. All retreats are held in silence apart from interview groups and meetings with the teachers. Group retreats vary in length from a weekend to nine days.

We also have facilities for personal retreats. The opportunity to spend time alone in a supportive environment dedicated to deepening understanding is rare and precious. Personal retreats are tailored to suit an individual's need.

In addition we offer work retreats for a minimum of two weeks, often at no charge.

Event Types
Guided group & individual retreats.

Subject Specialities
Meditation, reflection

Suitability
Adults.

Anne Ashton
Gaia House
West Ogwell
Newton Abbot
Devon
TQ12 6EN

☏ 01626 333613
📠 01626 352650
✉ enquiries@gaiahouse.co.uk

✔ **Retreat House**
✔ **Own Course Programme**

🛏 70 bedspaces.
🚍 By train or coach to Newton Abbot. Taxi or walk to Gaia House (approx 2 miles).

Focus Buddhist/Vipassana

South West England/Devon

Grimstone Manor

🔖 http://www.grimstonemanor.co.uk

Ron Pyatt
Grimstone Manor, Jordan Lane
Horrabridge, Yelverton
Devon PL20 7QY
✆ 01822 854358
✉ enquiries@
grimstonemanor.co.uk
✔ **Own Course Programme**
✔ **Venue for hire**
group full board (£44 to £48), large indoor space, several small spaces
🛏 40 bedspaces (1 single, 3 twins, 2 doubles, 7 family rooms).
🍽 Special diets.
♿ Wheelchair access.
🚆 Trains and coaches to Plymouth (National Rail: 0845 7484950; National Express Coaches: 0870 5808080). Local bus (0870 6082608) or Taxifast (01752 222222) to Horrabridge.

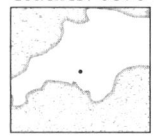

Grimstone Manor is a residential venue on the edge of Dartmoor, 9 miles north of Plymouth and 4 miles south of Tavistock. It is a very comfortable house with full central heating, an indoor swimming pool, jacuzzi and sauna.
Set in over 20 acres of grounds, the centre is run by a community helped by local people and occasional volunteers.
Food is mainly vegetarian and drinks and snacks are available in the dining room 24 hours a day. A good range of organic vegetarian wine is also available.
The Manor is open to courses all year; it is used regularly for courses in yoga, dance, healing, psychotherapy, massage and developmental training of numerous kinds, as well as offering a variety of holiday and working breaks.

Event Types
Guided group retreats, business retreats, own course programme, accredited courses, working holidays, regeneration programmes.

Subject Specialities
Inner process, group process, body & breathwork, ritual & shamanic, counselling, health & healing, alternative lifestyles & technology, self expression, conservation work, food & gardening, meditation.

Suitability or Specialism
Adults(++), couples(+), families with children(+), women, men, older people.

Focus
Eco-spiritual

Hawkwood

http://www.hawkwoodcollege.co.uk

A beautiful and peaceful setting. Situated at the head of a small Cotswold valley with panoramic views down to the Severn Vale. Comfortable accommodation. Well stocked library with log fire, large sitting room with piano. Extensive grounds host a wealth of flora and fauna, and a spring which provides drinking water. Walled organic garden supplies many ingredients for delicious meals. Within an Area of Outstanding Natural Beauty (AONB) with many miles of footpaths, and many lovely villages. Slad Valley (birthplace of author Laurie Lee), and Painswick with its famous churchyard are both nearby. Wide range of short courses including music, arts and crafts, and personal and spiritual development. While the spiritual impulse is the work of Rudolf Steiner, part of Hawkwood's mission is to bring anthroposophy into a fruitful interaction with other artistic and spiritual streams. This is reflected in the broad range of courses on offer.

Event Types
Guided group retreats, self directed retreats, business retreats, own course programme.

Subject Specialities
Music, Celtic studies, alternative lifestyles & technology, arts & crafts, body & breathwork, earth mysteries, group process, health & healing, inner process, meditation, prayer, ritual & shamanic, self expression ecology, educational training.

Suitability or Specialism
Adults and couples of all ages.

Katie
Hawkwood College
Painswick Old Road
Stroud
Gloucestershire
GL6 7LE
✆ 01453 759034
✆ 01453 764607
✉ info@hawkwoodcollege.co.uk

- ✔ **Retreat House**
- ✔ **Bed & Breakfast**
- ✔ **Own Course Programme**
- ✔ **Venue for hire**

🛏 51 bedspaces (14 singles, 17 twins).
🍽 Special diets.
♿ Wheelchair access.
🚂 Energetic 25 minute walk or taxi from Stroud railway station.

Focus Broadly Anthroposophical

Hazelwood House

Jane Bowman
Hazelwood House
Loddiswell
Kingsbridge
Devon
TQ7 4EB

✆ 01548 821232
✆ 01548 821318
✔ **Retreat House**
✔ **Bed & Breakfast**
✔ **Own Course Programme**
✔ **Venue for hire**
group full board (£40 to £70), large indoor space
⇝ 60 bedspaces (23 singles, 13 twins, 12 doubles, 3 family rooms).
🍽 Special diets.
♿ Wheelchair access.

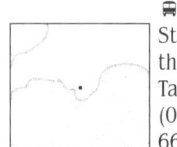

🚌 Totnes Station then Ray's Taxi Service (01803) 664567

Hazelwood, in the heart of the South Devonshire countryside, is a place of extraordinary peace and beauty. There are 67 acres of woodland, meadows, riverbank and orchards which are ideal for walking, painting or simply relaxing. Hazelwood is perfect for rest and reflection. Hazelwood House itself, which is early Victorian, is open 365 days a year. We offer accommodation and delicious food, mainly locally produced organic meat and vegetables freshly cooked for non-vegetarians and vegetarians alike. Guests may enjoy the comfort of log fires during the winter or relax on the veranda in summer. Four holiday cottages spread over the estate offer the possibility of self-catering accommodation. Concerts, cultural events and courses take place at Hazelwood throughout the year. We have a varied programme and would be pleased to put you on our mailing list. We have a licence to host civil weddings.

Event Types
Guided group retreats, self directed retreats, business retreats, own course programme.

Subject Specialities
Alternative lifestyles & technology, food & gardening, conservation work, health & healing, earth mysteries.

International Meditation Centre

http://www.imc-uk.org

The International Meditation Centre, UK, was founded in 1979 by the Sayagyi U Ba Khin Memorial Trust (registered under the Charities Act 1960) to provide for the instruction and practice of Theravada Buddhist Meditation. The Centre is a direct offspring of the International Meditation Centre of Yangon, Myanmar (formerly Rangoon, Burma), which was founded by Sayagyi U Ba Khin.

In addition to being a highly respected meditation teacher, Sayagyi U Ba Khin was the first Accountant General of Burma after Independence in 1948. The UK Centre is guided by Mother Sayamagyi, Sayagyi U Ba Khin's closest disciple, who has practised and taught meditation for the past fifty years and has carried on the tradition since Sayagyi U Ba Khin's demise in 1971. Ten-day residential courses led by Mother Sayamagyi or a regional teacher are normally held once a month beginning on Friday evening and ending early on Monday morning.

Event Types
Guided group retreats, own course programme.

Subject Specialities
Meditation, Theravada Buddhist Vipassana Meditation.

Suitability
Adults.

Splatts House
Heddington
Calne
Wiltshire
SN11 0PE

☎ 01380 850238
📠 01380 850238
✉ mail@imc-uk.org

✔ **Retreat House**
✔ **Own Course Programme**

🛏 30 bedspaces.
🍽 Vegetarian.

🚆 Train to Chippenham Station then taxi to Heddington

Focus Theravada Buddhist

South West England/Wiltshire

The Leela Centre

🌷 http://www.osholeela.co.uk

Veeren
Thorn Grove House
Common Mead Lane
Gillingham, Dorset
SP8 4RE

✆ 01747 821221
📠 01747 826386
✉ info@osholeela.co.uk

✓ **Venue for hire**
group full board (£33 to £50), large indoor space, several small spaces
🛏 72 bedspaces (13 doubles, 10 dormitories).
🍽 Exclusively vegetarian, special diets.
♿ Wheelchair access to ground floor.
🚌 National Express 1x daily London. London-Exeter mainline train to Gillingham (Dorset).

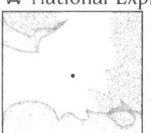

Focus Eastern

After four years near Wimborne, The Leela Centre, Britain's most vibrant and friendly centre moved to Gillingham (Dorset) in April 2000. It's a beautiful big house in wonderful north Dorset countryside. Leela also has its own registered caravan and camping park next door with excellent facilities. Leela is increasingly visited by people who want to relax, make friends and enjoy the atmosphere of celebration and naturalness. When featured on the BBC documentary 'Heaven and Earth' Toyah Wilcox was rapturously enthusiastic about the Leela Centre – "It's really fantastic. It's the first time I've opened up in 41 years". Situated between Stonehenge and Glastonbury, Leela's most popular programme is the monthly Super Special weekend, an introduction to the Leela community. On this low cost weekend, participants join the community in work, meditation, partying and hanging out. You are very welcome to come along and connect with our expanding network of life positive friends.

Event Types
Guided group retreats, own course programme, working holidays.

Subject Specialities
Self expression, group process, meditation, body & breathwork, health & healing, inner process, counselling.

Suitability or Specialism
Adults, couples, families with children, older people.

Eco-tourism features
Caravan and camping park. nature walk in 12 acres of new trees.

Little Burrows Centre

http://www.organicaccommodation.com

Little Burrows is situated in a peaceful and beautiful corner of Dartmoor, with nearby streams, rock pools, woodland walks and vast expanses of moorland with stone circles, rugged tors, singing skylarks and grazing ponies.

Kristin and Richard offer a quiet, beautiful, secluded place for retreats and creativity or an alternative holiday among like minded people. Accommodation consists of self-catering wooden cabins, caravan and rooms in house. All meals are all organic and vegetarian. Vegan, wheat free and other diets can be catered for.

Kristin and Richard are artists who also enjoy making music and offer a fully equipped recording studio with a grand piano for those wanting to make a CD and an art studio for those wanting to combine their holiday with something more creative. There is a mature garden with ponds and a waterfall, organic vegetable garden and wood burning sauna.

A place to just 'BE' and reconnect to one's innermost nature.

Food
Excl vegetarian, special diets.
Eco-tourism features
All food is organic, fresh herbs from the garden, home cooking. All cleaning products green, gardening organic, low energy lighting and heating.
Focus
All embracing

Kristin Charlesworth
Little Burrows Holiday & Retreat Centre
Shilstone Lane, Throwleigh
Okehampton EX20 2HX
✆ 01647 231305
✉ kristin@
organicaccommodation.com
✓ **Retreat House**
✓ **Bed & Breakfast**
✓ **Holiday Operator**
✓ **Own Course Programme**
✓ **Venue for hire**
group full board (£40 to £46) and self catering (£15 to £22), large indoor space and more
🛏 10 beds (4 sng, 4 twin, 4 dble, 2 fam, 3 cabins, 1 caravan).
♿ Wheelchair access.
🚆 Train/bus to Exeter: X9 or X10 to Whiddon Down then 2 mile walk.
We can pick up from Exeter or Whiddon Down.

South West England/Devon

Lower Shaw Farm

🔖 http://www.lowershawfarm.co.uk

Andrea Hirsch or Matt Holland
Lower Shaw Farm
Old Shaw Lane, Shaw
Swindon SN5 5PJ
✆ 01793 771080
📠 01793 771080
✉ enquiries@
lowershawfarm.co.uk

✔ **Bed & Breakfast**
✔ **Own Course Programme**
✔ **Venue for hire**

group full board (£30), several small spaces

🛏 30 bedspaces (7 singles, 4 doubles, 7 family rooms, 4 dormitories).
🍽 Exclusively vegetarian, special diets.
♿ Wheelchair access to most of farm.

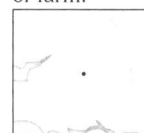

🚆 Train to Swindon then short local bus ride.

Focus Humanist

Lower Shaw Farm offers weekend breaks, working and learning holidays, as well as opportunities for volunteering. Typically, our programme includes craft courses such as willow basket and felt making, organic gardening and wholefood cookery, yoga, walking with nature, and African drumming. There is an annual literature festival, a juggling and circus skills holiday, a singing and music weekend, and seasonal Family Activity Holidays. The farm is also available for hire by groups and conference organisers.

Once a dairy farm deep in rural North Wiltshire, Lower Shaw Farm now has another life: as a three-acre oasis in an area of 1980s development. The farm has kept a character and atmosphere of its own, with organic gardens, living willow structures, ponds, poultry, sheep, a campfire circle, and play spaces for both children and adults. Lower Shaw is run by a family of five with a network of helpers, local, national, and international.

The outbuildings have been converted into meeting rooms, workshops, and accommodation, much of which is accessible to people with disabilities - please ask for details. The accommodation is basic, but homely. There is a visitors' kitchen for drinks and snacks, and small and large group rooms. The organic vegetarian meals are prepared with mostly homegrown and locally produced ingredients. Not far away is Avebury and the Ridgeway.

Programme of courses, and hire/B&B charges, available on request. We welcome telephone enquiries. Life is for learning at Lower Shaw Farm!

… http://www.themagdalenproject.org.uk

The Magdalen Project

Experience the Magdalen Project, a safe and inspiring environment for a wide variety of purposes, including ecological education, conferences, seminars, training sessions, team building and craft and healing residentials. Set on a 132 acre organic farm in the lush splendour of the Somerset and Dorset borders, the centre provides the ideal setting for creative training, reflective learning or simply unwinding and relaxing. The focus of our centre is an attractive courtyard of old stone and brick farm buildings which have been converted to provide accommodation for a wide range of purposes. Accompanied children can be accommodated.

Event Types
Own course programme.

Subject Specialities
Ecological education, team building, conservation work, outdoor activities & sport, food & gardening.

Eco-tourism features
Organic smallholding with vegetables, fruit and traditional breeds. Rich and varied environment with range of carefully managed habitats.

Sigrun Appleby
Magdalen Farm
Winsham
Chard
Somerset
TA20 4PA

✆ 01460 30144
✆ 01460 30177
✉ wessex@themagdalenproject.org.uk

✓ **Retreat House**
✓ **Own Course Programme**
✓ **Venue for hire**

⇌ 35 bedspaces.
🍽 Special diets.
♿ Full wheelchair access.

South West England/Dorset

Middle Piccadilly Healing Centre

http://www.middlepiccadilly.com

Dominic Harvey
Middle Piccadilly
Holwell
Sherborne
Dorset
DT9 5LW

℡ 01963 23468
✆ 01963 23764
✉ info@middlepiccadilly.com

✔ **Retreat House**
✔ **Bed & Breakfast**
✔ **Own Course Programme**
✔ **Venue for hire**

🛏 9 bedspaces (3 singles, 1 twin, 2 doubles).
🍴 Exclusively vegetarian.
🚆 Sherbourne Station then taxi (with Beaver Cabs 01935 816620) to Middle Piccadilly

Experience the magic of Middle Piccadilly - The Alternative Health Farm Middle Piccadilly is a fully residential Natural Healing Centre established in September 1986, the building itself is a 17th Century thatched country house and stable wing lovingly converted and attractively furnished to provide accommodation for up to 9 residents. The surrounding Dorset countryside is especially beautiful, the peaceful and tranquil atmosphere is almost tangible at the centre. It is first and foremost a place of healing, the purpose of the centre is to provide a welcoming and informal atmosphere, where guests feel totally at home. The centre offers a residential programme of Wholistic Health Intensives which include an extensive range of alternative therapies and specialist baths that help to relieve our guests of all the pressures and stresses of modern life and promote the process of self healing.

Event Types
Guided individual and self directed retreats, business retreats, own courses.

Subject Specialities
Health & healing, alternative medicine.

Suitability or Specialism
Adults(+), couples(+), women(+), men(+), older people(+).

Monkton Wyld Court

http://www.monktonwyldcourt.org

Our Centre for Holistic Education offers an exciting and varied programme of residential courses, ranging from shamanism and fire walking, to qigong and Tibetan healing exercises, to retreats and environmental workcamps; plus the ever-popular Family Weeks throughout the year. We also offer accommodation for B&B/full board whenever possible.

The centre is run by a friendly, live-in community of 12-16 adults plus children and cats, with help from visiting volunteers. The setting is a neo-gothic Victorian rectory and outbuildings placed in a beautiful Dorset valley three miles from the sea at Lyme Regis. The 11 acre estate comprises a small farm, a walled organic vegetable garden, terraced lawns, children's play area, woods and a stream. The house sleeps up to 35 guests and includes two large group rooms, piano room, library, meditation hut, healing room, craft shop, pottery and arts facilities. So come and discover, escape, relax or whatever you need to do.

Event Types
Guided group retreats, own course programme, working holidays.

Subject Specialities
Family, yoga, meditation, ritual & shamanic, health & healing, body & breathwork, inner process, conservation work, arts & crafts, alternative lifestyles & technology.

Suitability or Specialism
Adults, families with children.

Abbie James
Monkton Wyld, Charmouth
Bridport, Dorset
DT6 6DQ
✆ 01297 560342
✆ 01297 560395
✉ monktonwyldcourt@btinternet.com
✓ **Bed & Breakfast**
✓ **Own Course Programme**
✓ **Venue for hire**
group full board (£37 to £42), large indoor space, several small spaces
🛏 35 bedspaces (3 twins, 1 double, 8 dormitories)
🍴 Exclusively vegetarian, special diets.
♿ No wheelchair access.
🚌 Axminster railway station 4 miles away. Taxi, or Bus 31 to Hunters Lodge followed by 1 mile walk.

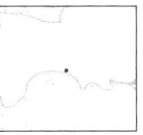

South West England/Dorset

St Peter's Grange

🔗 http://www.stpetersgrange-prinknash.com

Robert & Mary Jones
St Peter's Grange
Prinknash Abbey, Cranham,
Gloucester GL4 8EX
✆ 01452 813592
📠 01452 814187
✉ spgprinknash@freeuk.com
✔ **Retreat House**
✔ **Venue for hire**
group full board (£35 to £37), large indoor space and more

🛏 33 bedspaces (3 singles, 4 doubles with additional singles, 2 twins, 4 family rooms).
🍽 Special diets.
♿ Portable ramps inside, over 2 flights of 2 steps each. Exterior access/exit 1 step only. Ground floor accomm.
🚌 Stroud-Cheltenham bus hourly in both directions.

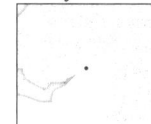

Alight Cranham Corner, cross to half-timbered lodge, down hill inside estate

A 16th century house of prayer in 500 acres of Cotswold parkland with views across the Severn valley towards the Malvern Hills. It is an extension of the Abbey Guest Wing (men only) but for everyone. Guests are invited to join the Community in the Abbey Church for Services (five a day).

The Grange is also open to any group for residential or day retreats. Accommodation is comfortable though simple with hot and cold water in all rooms and separate shower/bathrooms. There are four spacious sitting rooms, a chapel, a dining room seating 50 and simple home cooking with attention to any special dietary needs. No smoking in the building.

Except for four led Days of Recollection each year, groups are normally hosted here and bring their own retreat director with them. Exceptionally, however, Father Abbot may be contacted to request a leader from the Community if a group is unable to supply its own.

Events
Led Days (and or weekends) of Recollection, self-directed retreats, hosting of group retreats with their own programme. Suitable for adults, couples, families with children and older people.

Focus Christian/Catholic

http://www.samwaysfarm.co.uk

Samways Farm

Samways Farm is a beautiful complex of listed buildings situated in the Cranborne Chase designated Area of Outstanding Natural Beauty. The farm has been used as a location in several period films including Thomas Hardy's "The Woodlanders".

The farmhouse has three lovely en-suite twin rooms for B&B and there are also two comfortable self-catering cottages, each sleeping four, and a Shepherd's Hut with a double bed. It is a wonderful place for walking, cycling, riding, bird watching or just taking it easy and there are plenty of interesting sites to explore locally – Salisbury, Bath, Stonehenge, Avebury, the stunning World Heritage Dorset coastline. Within the farm courtyard is a converted eighteenth century stone barn with wooden floor (19'6" x 56'6") that can be used for celebrations and workshops and there are two good-sized rooms in the house (17'6" x 20' with open fireplace and 15'6" x 22'6" with wood burner). We run our own yoga, walking and riding holidays but welcome enquires from those who wish to hire the facilities for their own group or workshop.

Claire Morris
Samways Farm
Alvediston
Salisbury
Wiltshire
SP5 5LQ

✆ 01722 780286
✉ claire@samwaysfarm.co.uk

✔ **Bed & Breakfast**
✔ **Own Course Programme**
✔ **Venue for hire**

⌁ 16 bedspaces (3 twins, 2 self-catering cottages, 1 shepherd's hut)
🍽 Exclusively vegetarian, special diets.
🚆 Train to Tisbury (5 miles) or Salisbury (13 miles) then taxi or infrequent bus.

South West England/Wiltshire

Sancreed House

🌐 http://www.sancreedhouse.com

Clare Dyas
Sancreed House
Sancreed
Penzance, Cornwall
TR20 8QS

📞 01736 810409
✉ claredyas@madasafish.com

✔ **Retreat House**
✔ **Bed & Breakfast**
✔ **Holiday Operator**
✔ **Own Course Programme**
✔ **Venue for hire**
group full board (£30 to £45), group self catering (£10 to £15), large indoor space

🛏 10 bedspaces (1 single, 1 double, 3 twins).
🍽 Exclusively vegetarian, special diets.

🚉 Penzance Station then bus 9.
Focus
Eclectic

Sancreed House is in an area of spiritual tradition dating back to Celtic times when St Credan lived beside a nearby holy well. It was a vicarage for many centuries since the Domesday Book though it has been renovated since .
We are a small loose-knit community and offer a peaceful space where people can unwind relax and explore themselves and/or the beautiful Cornish countryside, coastal walks and ancient sites.
There is a self-contained chalet for quiet weeks in the gardens which are subtropical and unusual.
We offer a meditation space and also the use of art studios and tuition in painting, pottery or wood sculpture by arrangement.
We also offer spiritual healing, massage, counselling, regression, astrology, art therapy and animal healing. All people welcome. Retreats seeking recuperation, change of direction or life change.
We can be flexible and accommodate various arrangements for people singly or in groups, in 1 double room, 3 twins and a chalet. We can accommodate about 10 people. B&B £20 single £35 double. Full Board £40 per day single. Vegetarian Food. Self-catering Chalet £70 per week.

Eco-tourism features
Many ancient sites nearby including holy well. Beautiful peaceful sub-tropical garden

Self Realization Meditation Healing Centre

http://www.selfrealizationcentres.org

The Centre is a charitable trust founded by Mata Yoganandaji to help people – of all beliefs and none – find peace and fulfillment. Run by a spiritual family of teachers, healers and counsellors, providing courses, individual appointments, retreats and nurturing breaks, it is a spiritual home in every sense – with unconditional love as the watchword. Pure Meditation courses are held regularly and all are welcome to join the morning and evening meditations. There are three acres of beautiful gardens, log fires in winter, a library and therapy pool. Home-cooked vegetarian meals – special diets catered for. Please ask for a colour brochure and full course programme, including Pure Meditation courses, Professional Healer and Counsellor Training, Self Development, Hatha and Aqua Yoga and Teacher Training courses.

Event Types
Guided group retreats, guided individual retreats, self directed retreats, business retreats, own course programme, accredited courses, teacher training, regeneration programmes.

Subject Specialities
Meditation, body & breathwork, counselling, group process, health & healing, inner process, prayer, self expression, Hatha Yoga.

Eco-tourism features
Garden retreat chalet accommodation with ecological Bio-Let toilet. Organic homegrown vegetables and salad (where possible).

Mariananda Azaz
Self Realization Meditation Healing Centre, Laurel Lane
Queen Camel, Yeovil
Somerset BA22 7NU

✆ 01935 850266
✆ 01935 850234
info@
selfrealizationcentres.org

✔ **Retreat House**
✔ **Own Course Programme**
↪ 31 bedspaces (7 twins, 2 family rooms).
🍽 Special diets.
♿ New teaching room (for 2004) has disabled access.
🚂 Approximately 5 miles from both Castle Cary and Sherborne railway stations. Taxis available and we are sometimes able to collect guests.
Focus All welcome

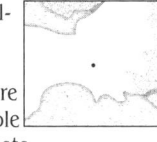

Shambhala Health & Healing Retreat

http://www.shambhala.co.uk

Isis Livingstone
Shambhala
Coursing Batch
Glastonbury
Somerset
BA6 8BH

☏ 01458 831797
✆ 01458 834751
✉ findyourself@shambhala.co.uk

- ✔ **Retreat House**
- ✔ **Bed & Breakfast**
- ✔ **Holiday Operator**
- ✔ **Own Course Programme**

🛏 11 bedspaces (1 single, 2 twins, 2 doubles).
🍽 Exclusively vegetarian, special diets.
🚌 Castle Cary station (1½ hours from London Paddington) then taxi (12 miles).

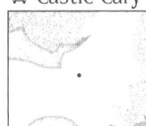

Focus Love

Spacious, sunny, comfortable rooms – Egyptian, Chinese, Tibetan, Dove, Blossom and Star – some en-suite, some with balcony. Beautiful gardens with ponds and waterfalls and a flock of white peace doves. Superb massage, Bowen technique, vortex healing, LaStone hot and cold massage therapy, detoxing, use of jacuzzi and sauna. Spiritual awakening, heart opening and higher consciousness experiences. Great organic, vegetarian food. Shambhala is an island of tranquillity in the sea of confusion. It is a retreat for contemplation, for physical and emotional healing, for spiritual renewal and growth, or simply a place to relax and let go of the world. Ideal for visiting groups. On the slopes of Glastonbury Tor, it is a sacred site, with a crystal star, meditation spaces, a sanctuary and a lot of laughter. Space and time to relax and heal.
"Once you walk through the gate and cross the crystal star set in the stones, the whole garden and house become a green and gentle sanctuary away from the world." *Good Retreat Guide* Gold Star Award
"It's a place to go when life's big questions are whirling through the mind ... very genuine vibe of goodwill and gentleness" *Vogue Magazine*
"Shambhala curls itself around you like a warm rug. It would take a strange person not to experience pleasure and well-being here." *Independent on Sunday*
Voted one of the Top Ten Retreats in the UK by the *Daily Mail* AA Double Diamond Certification

Event Types
Self directed retreats, own course programme.
Subject Specialities
Personal empowerment, spiritual development, body & breathwork, counselling, health & healing, meditation, inner process.

🕮 http://www.shekinashram.org

Shekinashram

Shekinashram is a newly formed community and dedicated sacred space, situated at the base of Chalice Hill, on a pilgrimage route to Glastonbury Tor. There are currently five permanent residents at the ashram. We are open all year round and welcome guests to join us in this inspirational, transformative space.

Essentially the vision of the Shekinashram is to express a way of life that is both conscious and selfless, and which deeply honours the One in all its miraculous forms. We live according to a set of holistic principles, and maintain the ashram in a spacious way that is intentionally free from unnecessary distractions. This environment is naturally conducive to the development of spiritual practise and the cultivation of internal disciplines. It is intended that this way of life genuinely reflects freedom of Being. We promote an abundant and sustainable lifestyle, enjoy an organic vegan raw food diet, meditate, practice yoga and sing devotional songs together. A commitment to living Self-Realisation and a willingness to enter into profound relationship underpins our being together.

We have a group room for hire, and are able to accommodate up to 10 guests on residential workshops. We also have bed and breakfast accommodation available for short and longer term paying guests, and a growing programme of events, workshops, and retreats. We also offer morning meditation, one to one therapeutic treatments, raw food lunches, fresh juices, sauna and office facilities.

Event Types
Healing breaks, cleansing retreats, weekend courses, guided group & self directed retreats, own course programme, evening groups, daily meditation, devotional singing.

Subject Specialities
Spiritual development, meditation, raw food nutrition, health & healing, group & inner process.

Elahn
Shekinashram
Dod Lane, Glastonbury
Somerset BA6 8BZ
✆ 01458 832300
🖂 info@shekinashram.org
✔ **Retreat House**
✔ **Own Course Programme**
🛏 Maximum 10 bed spaces. B&B (£15 sharing - £25 single - £45 twin or double - £65 double en-suite) or full board. No smoking or alcohol in house or garden. 32 x 16 foot group room for hire. Sauna & office facilities.
🍽 Exclusively vegan raw food.
🚍 Local bus from Bath/Bristol to Glastonbury or train to Castle Cary, then a 20 min taxi journey. 5 minutes walk from Glastonbury town centre. 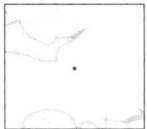
Focus Eco-Spiritual/Non-dualistic

Tordown

🕸 http://www.tordown.com

Sherhadasha and Michael Penn
5 Ashwell Lane
Glastonbury
Somerset
BA6 8BG

✆ 01458 832287
✆ 01458 831100
✉ torangel@aol.com

✔ **Retreat House**
✔ **Bed & Breakfast**
✔ **Own Course Programme**

🛏 14 bedspaces (2 singles, 2 twins, 1 double, 2 family rooms).
🍽 Exclusively vegetarian.
🚆 Train to Castle Cary then 20 minute taxi ride. Buses from Bath, Bristol or London.

Situated on the southern slopes of the Tor overlooking the Vale of Avalon. Television, basin, tea and coffee making facilities in all rooms, with many en suite. Vegetarian, no smoking, own car park, garden, patio with glorious views, waterfall and pond. Two Reiki Masters in residence. Also available: Ear Candeling; Higher Self Communication Sessions; Hydrotherapy pool; Multi-dimensional Cellular healing; Reset and Whole Health Body Scans; Massage can be arranged. Family run with a welcoming, friendly, peaceful and spiritual atmosphere. Varied accommodation. Choose from our Citrene, Clear Quartz, Amethyst, Malachite Lapis and Rose Quartz rooms or our Angelic Opal suites. Library containing some of the oldest and newest spiritual/healing books. A place to be peaceful, refind yourself, relax and enjoy. English Tourist Board: 4 diamonds.

Event Types
Guided group retreats, guided individual retreats, self directed retreats, own course programme, teacher training.

Subject Specialities
Health & healing, inner process.

Suitability or Specialism
Adults.

🕸 http://www.trevina.com

Trevina House

Whether you are coming to Trevina to try sustainable living, practice organic gardening or just receive some well-earned peace and quiet, then you have found the right place. We must, however, admit that Trevina can be a little noisy – there is the constant background rumble of the little waterfall on the River Loveney where it flows under an old bridge lower down the valley. Then, if there is a southerly breeze the chimes from the church clock tower a mile away and 200 feet below us can hourly disturb the solitude, and Wednesday night is bell-ringing practice ...
Meanwhile buzzards with their mournful mewing drift across the valley most afternoons and all through autumn and winter evenings owls calling in the woods echo far into the night. In June there may even be the high decibel activity of two nightingales serenading each other (or squabbling over territory) from a pair of beech trees in the garden. From the first cuckoo to when "... gathering swallows twitter in the skies", the seasons at Trevina merge seamlessly one to another, in memory of what has gone and anticipation of that to come, an endless present.
One often hears of gardeners suffering vandalism, we also have our fair share. Badgers each year assist us in digging our potatoes, deer prune our orchard trees (not when or where we need pruning) and blackbirds eat our raspberries and strawberries. Pity too the poor farmers around here who can all relate stories of the occasional loss of lamb or sheep (or hanging half side of pork) to the nocturnal visitations of Leo padus, mythical to DEFRA but real enough when one crosses the road in front of the car at 11.00pm! With no street lamps or nearby towns the nights are very dark, just the Milky Way and the silvery moon to light your path. We love Trevina House and the myths and legends that abound in this part of Cornwall. All this is yours to share.

Eco-tourism features
Organic gardening and food, Permaculture.

Sue Wright
Trevina
St Neot
Liskeard
Cornwall
PL14 6NR

✆ 01579 321359
📠 01579 321359
✉ mail@trevina.com

✔ **Bed & Breakfast**
✔ **Own Course Programme**
🛏 Maximum 6 guests (2 doubles, 1 twin, 1 single). Individual B&B £20-£23/person. No smoking in house.
🍽 Traditional B&B catering, full board exclusively vegetarian, meals taken refectory style, special diets catered for.
Focus All welcome with mutual respect and understanding

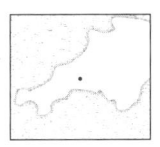

South West England/Cornwall

Wild Pear Centre

↓ http://www.primalintegration.com

Juliana Brown
Wild Pear Centre, King Street
Combe Martin
Devon
EX34 0AG

℗ 020 8341 7226
✆ 020 8341 7226
🖰 wildpearinfo@
primalintegration.com

✓ **Retreat House**
✓ **Venue for hire**
group full board (£30 to £35), large indoor space, several small spaces
⌂ 25 bedspaces (3 twins, 2 doubles, 5 dormitories).
🍽 Special diets.
🚆 Train to Barnstaple then bus or taxi to Combe Martin, alternatively coach to Ilfracombe then bus or taxi

A centre for personal growth work located in a seaside village on the edge of Exmoor National Park and close to spectacular coastal scenery and secluded beaches. With a large group room and communal hall, generously equipped with cushions, work mattresses and a piano, the centre is a suitable workshop venue for a variety of group activities such as yoga, meditation, growth groups, bodywork, movement and dance. Available for hire for residential or non-residential use (full board or self-catered) at reasonable rates, the centre also welcomes individual or group retreats or groups on holiday.

Event Types
Guided group retreats, self directed retreats.

Subject Specialities
Body & breathwork, counselling, earth mysteries, group process, health & healing, inner process, meditation, ritual & shamanic, self expression.

Suitability or Specialism
Adults.

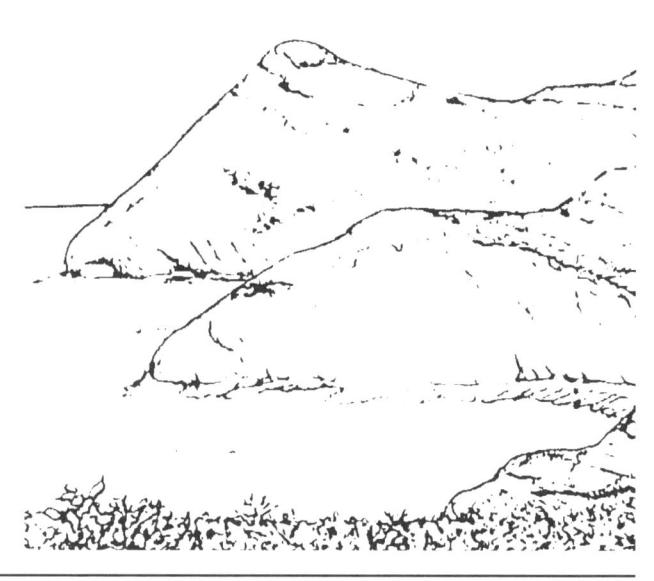

Places to BE 2004/Page 92

South West England/Devon

Other Places and Organisations

Adventureline
North Trefula Farm
Redruth
Cornwall
TR16 5ET
Holiday Operator

Ashton Lodge
Stanbridge
Wimborne
Dorset
BH21 4JQ
Venue for Hire

Berachah Colour Healing Centre
Well House Lane
Glastonbury
Somerset
BA6 8BJ
Bed & Breakfast

Boswell Farm
Sidford
Sidmouth
Devon
EX10 0PP
Venue for Hire

Burton Bradstock Othona Community
Community House
Coast Road
Burton Bradstock
Bridport
Dorset
DT6 4RN
Retreat House

C A E R
Rosemerryn
Lamorna
Penzance
Cornwall
TR19 6BN
Own Course Programme

Chalice Well Trust
Chilkwell Street
Glastonbury
Somerset
BA6 8DD
Retreat House

Chy Gwella
53 Morrab Road
Penzance
Cornwall
TR18 4EX
Bed & Breakfast

Cowden House
Frys Lane
Godmanstone
Dorchester
DT2 7AG
Bed & Breakfast
☏ 01300 341377

Croydon Hall
Rodhuish
Minehead
Somerset
TA24 6QT
Venue for Hire

Other Places and Organisations

Devon Health Spa at Rosehill
30 West Hill
Budleigh Salterton
Devon
EX9 6BU
Retreat House

Fern Tor Vegetarian and Vegan Guest House
Meshaw
South Molton
Devon
EX36 4NA
Bed & Breakfast

Gara Rock
East Portlemouth
Salcombe
Devon
TQ8 8PH
Bed & Breakfast

Gaunts House
Wimborne
Dorset
BH21 4JQ
Own Course Programme

Hamilton Hall
1 Carysfort Road
Boscombe
Bournemouth
Dorset
BH1 4EJ
Own Course Programme

Hazel Hill Woodland Retreat Centre
care of Garden Lodge
Winchester Road
Kings Somborne
Stockbridge
SO20 6NY
Own Course Programme
✆ 01794 388707
✉ hazelhill@workingvision.com

Home Place
Home Place Farm
Challacombe
Barnstaple
Devon
EX31 4TS
Bed & Breakfast

School of the Living Light
Millslade Hall
Station Road
Ashcott
Bridgwater
Somerset
TA7 9QP
Own Course Programme

Making Waves Vegan Guesthouse
3 Richmond Place
St Ives
Cornwall
TR26 1JN
Bed & Breakfast

Marlborough House
1 Marlborough Lane
Bath
Somerset
BA1 2NQ
Bed & Breakfast

Other Places and Organisations

Marridge Hill Cottage
Marridge Hill
Ramsbury
Marlborough
Wiltshire
SN8 2HG
Bed & Breakfast

Mount Pleasant Farm
Gorran High Lanes
St Austell
Cornwall
PL26 6LR
Retreat House

Pilsdon Community
Pilsdon Manor
Bridport
Dorset
DT6 5NZ
Retreat House

Pitt White
Mill Lane
Uplyme
Lyme Regis
Dorset
DT7 3TZ
Venue for Hire

Prebendal Farm
Bishopstone
Swindon, Wiltshire
SN6 8PT
Bed & Breakfast

Schumacher College
The Old Postern
Dartington
Totnes, Devon
TQ9 6EA
Own Course Programme

The Sheldon Centre
Dunsford
Exeter
Devon
EX6 7LE
Venue for Hire

Tribe of Doris
26 Albany Road
Montpelier
Bristol
BS6 5LH
Own Course Programme

Whitesands Lodge
Sennen
Penzance
Cornwall
TR19 7AR
Venue for Hire

Woodstock
Lee
Ilfracombe
Devon
EX34 8LN
© 01271 879477

The Yarner Trust
Welcombe Barton
Welcombe
Bideford
Devon
EX39 6HG
Venue for Hire

South East England

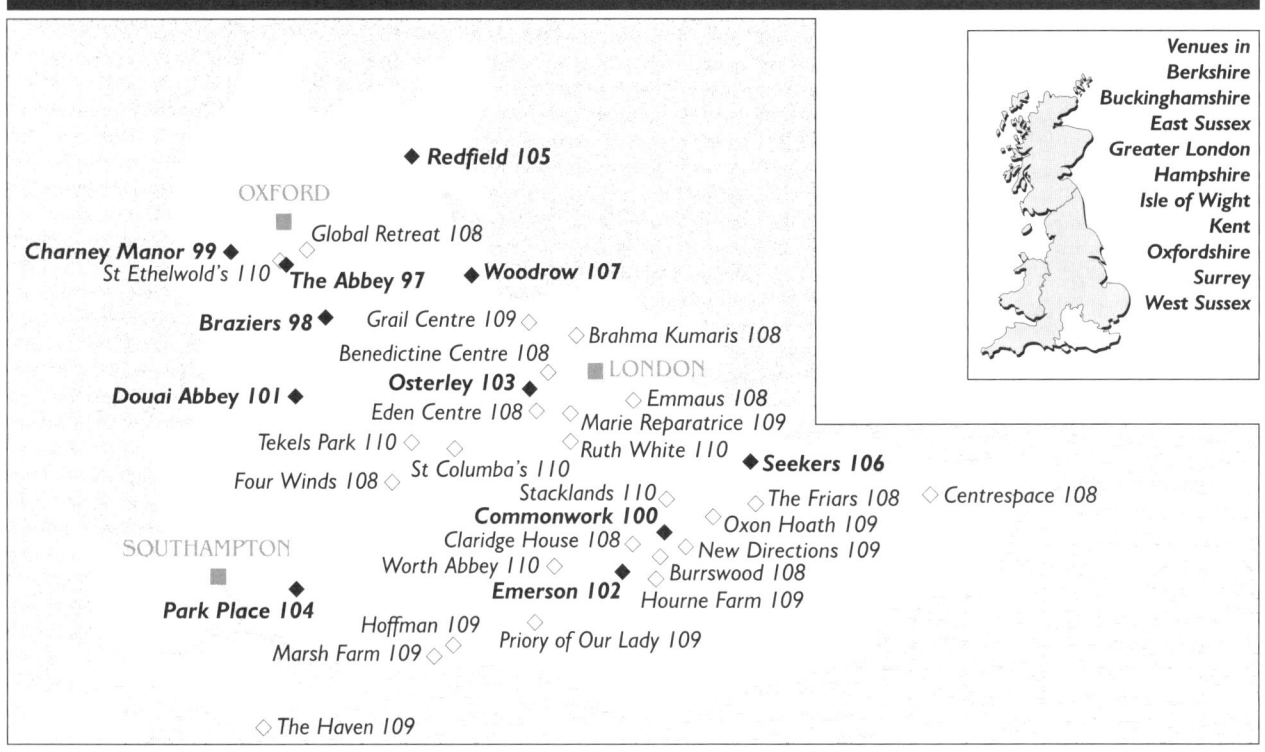

♦ Redfield 105

OXFORD

◇ Global Retreat 108

♦ Charney Manor 99
◇ St Ethelwold's 110 ♦ The Abbey 97 ♦ Woodrow 107

♦ Braziers 98 ◇ Grail Centre 109
◇ Benedictine Centre 108 ◇ Brahma Kumaris 108
♦ Osterley 103 LONDON
♦ Douai Abbey 101 ◇ Eden Centre 108 ◇ Emmaus 108
◇ Marie Reparatrice 109
◇ Tekels Park 110 ◇ Ruth White 110 ♦ Seekers 106
◇ Four Winds 108 ◇ St Columba's 110 ◇ The Friars 108 ◇ Centrespace 108
◇ Stacklands 110 ◇ Oxon Hoath 109
♦ Commonwork 100 ◇ New Directions 109
◇ Claridge House 108 ◇ Burrswood 108
◇ Worth Abbey 110 ♦ Emerson 102 ◇ Hourne Farm 109

SOUTHAMPTON

♦ Park Place 104
◇ Hoffman 109
◇ Marsh Farm 109 ◇ Priory of Our Lady 109

◇ The Haven 109

Venues in
Berkshire
Buckinghamshire
East Sussex
Greater London
Hampshire
Isle of Wight
Kent
Oxfordshire
Surrey
West Sussex

Places to BE 2004/Page 96

The Abbey

🔹 http://www.theabbey.uk.com

The Abbey is a retreat and education centre housed in a 13th Century buildings and four acres of peaceful grounds. Rooted in the Christian tradition and open to the wisdom of other faiths, the Abbey provides a setting for the exploration of deep spiritual truths and values and the mystery of life. The community based at the Abbey, locally and further afield, holds a sacred space, open to this universal quest for truth.

The beauty and tranquillity of the house and grounds invite contemplation and a stilling of the inner. The challenges of living within an honest community of people whilst running a thriving education and retreat centre also encourage active engagement with the realities of modern life. We hold a welcome for all who are seeking to live life inspired by spirit.

Event Types
Guided group & self directed retreats, business retreats, own course programme.

Subject Specialities
Group process, inner process, meditation, self expression, community living, emergent spirituality.

Eco-tourism features
The Abbey is just off the Sustrans cycle route No 5 between Oxford and Didcot.

Cliff
The Abbey
Sutton Courtenay
Abingdon
Oxfordshire
OX14 4AF
✆ 01235 847401
📠 01235 847608
✉ admin@theabbeysc.demon.co.uk

✔ **Retreat House**
✔ **Bed & Breakfast**
✔ **Own Course Programme**
✔ **Venue for hire**

group full board (£35 to £50), large indoor space, several small spaces

🛏 18 bedspaces (6 singles.)
🍽 Exclusively vegetarian.
🚌 Didcot Station then bus 32 to The Triangle, Sutton Courtenay (or taxi – about £7)

Focus Inter-faith

South East England/Oxfordshire

Braziers Park

🌐 http://www.braziers.org.uk

Maurice Roth
Braziers Park
Ipsden
Wallingford
Oxfordshire
OX10 6AN

☎ 01491 680221
📠 01491 680221
✉ admin@braziers.org.uk

✔ **Retreat House**
✔ **Own Course Programme**
✔ **Venue for hire**

🛏 31 bedspaces (3 singles, 4 twins, 3 doubles, 4 family rooms.)
🍽 Special diets.
🚕 Taxi from Goring & Streatley Railway Station.

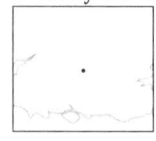

Braziers Park was founded in 1950 as a practical centre to study humankind's place in the world. It is run by a resident group, and volunteers who donate their services. Braziers is set in 50 acres of graceful Chiltern countryside, with pasture and woodland, in an area of outstanding natural beauty. The main house itself is Grade 2* listed and is complemented by numerous outbuildings. Braziers estate is organic and the walled kitchen garden provides much of the produce for the house in season. Cooking is substantially, but not exclusively, vegetarian. The atmosphere is relaxed and informal.

Event Types
Guided group retreats, guided individual retreats, self directed retreats, business retreats, own course programme, working holidays.

Subject Specialities
Alternative lifestyles & technology, group process, food & gardening, arts & crafts, self expression, conservation work, ritual & shamanic, meditation, outdoor activities & sport, body & breathwork.

Suitability or Specialism
Adults, couples, women, men, older people.

Eco-tourism features
Permaculture

Charney Manor

http://www.charneymanor.demon.co.uk

Charney Manor, one of the oldest inhabited houses in Britain, is a place of tranquillity, where people come for reflection, renewal and retreat. Once the grange of the Benedictine abbey of Abingdon, the Manor is now owned and managed by Quakers (Friends). With its comfortable rooms and delightful grounds the Manor offers a warm welcome to visitors throughout the year. As well as conferences and training events for religious and other groups, Charney hosts its own programme of courses which reflects current and emerging concerns amongst Quakers. The courses in our programme seek to nourish the spirit through silence, listening deeply and exploring with heart and mind. Fourteen en-suite rooms, two of which are suitable for disabled people.

Event Types
Guided group retreats, self directed retreats, business retreats, own course programme, day bookings.

Subject Specialities
Inner process, arts & crafts, self expression, health & healing, meditation, prayer, earth mysteries, literature.

Suitability
Adults(+), older people.

The Manager
Charney Manor
Charney Bassett
Wantage
Oxfordshire
OX12 0EJ

☏ 01235 868206
✆ 01235 868882
✉ charneymanor@quaker.org.uk

✓ **Retreat House**
✓ **Own Course Programme**
✓ **Venue for hire**

group full board (£54 to £59.50), large indoor space, several small spaces

🛏 43 bedspaces (13 singles, 15 twins, 2 family rooms.)
🍽 Special diets.
♿ Wheelchair access.
🚆 Train to Didcot Parkway then 20 minute taxi journey.
Focus Quaker

The Commonwork Centre

🌐 http://www.commonwork.org

Centre Administrator
Bore Place, Chiddingstone
Edenbridge
TN8 7AR
☎ 01732 463255 x229
📠 01732 740264
✉ info@commonwork.org
✔ **Retreat House**
✔ **Own Course Programme**
✔ **Venue for hire**
group full board (£72.85 to £119.85), group self catering (£42.30 to £48.18), large indoor & several small spaces
🛏 45 bedspaces (7 singles, 15 twins, 3 family rooms). Camping by arrangement.
♿ Two meeting rooms and some residential accommodation are wheelchair accessible.
🚆 Train to Sevenoaks then taxi from station forecourt to Bore Place.

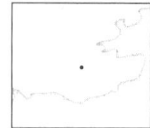

Commonwork, an educational trust, is a place for conferences, workshops and seminars on a 500-acre organic farm in the beautiful Kentish low Weald, near Sevenoaks. An old manor house (listed Grade II), with its ancient walled garden, and a group of historic barns within a courtyard, have been sensitively renovated to provide a restful but creative environment.
Our variety of spaces means that we can accommodate small or large groups in comfort and with privacy, up to approx. 45 residents or 4 to 100 people for daytime visits. Each group has exclusive use of their space during their visit to undertake their own work or retreat. We can also arrange Commonwork tutors for group activities such as claywork, guided walks, night walks, breadmaking and green woodwork. Our spaces are also suitable for dance, music and drama.
We have just launched a new annual 'natural garden' programme, which includes a 24- and a 48-hour retreat. Please phone or email for details.
Our field trail through farmland and woodland - with 25 ponds - can be walked at any time and we also have a mini-field trail at the heart of the site which is wheelchair accessible.

Please do not hesitate to contact us about your specific requirements and budget. Prices are negotiable for not-for-profit groups.
Food
Delicious meals, using local and organic ingredients where possible; self catering groups welcomed. Licensed for wine and beer, Fairtrade tea and coffee.
Eco-tourism features
We run environmental education, garden and conservation programmes.

Places to BE 2004/Page 100

South East England/Kent

Douai Abbey

🏛 http://www.douaiabbey.org.uk

A Benedictine monastery offering hospitality and day conference facilities to individuals, small groups and workshops; also an organised retreat programme. Situated on the North Wessex Downs in an area of outstanding natural beauty. Good network of footpaths for walking. A variety of accommodation, some en suite. Meals are provided. Also available is hostel type self-catering accommodation. Further information about staying and about our retreat and workshop programme can be obtained from the 'Programme Director'. Good rail and road connections: M4 exit 12 is 6 miles: railway station Midgham on Paddington to Newbury line is 1 mile. Oxford, Stonehenge and Winchester all within an hour's drive.

Event Types
Guided group retreats, self directed retreats, business retreats, own course programme.

Subject Specialities
Meditation, prayer.

Suitability or Specialism
Adults(+), couples(+), families with children, women, men, young people 12 to 17, children under 12, older people.

Father Oliver Holt
Douai Abbey
Upper Woolhampton
Reading, Berkshire
RG7 5TQ
☏ 0118 971 5399
✆ 0118 971 5303
✉ info@douaiabbey.org.uk

✔ **Retreat House**
✔ **Own Course Programme**
✔ **Venue for hire**
group full board (£35 to £43), large indoor space, several small spaces

↪ 46 bedspaces (18 singles, 2 twins, 1 double, 1 family room, 5 dormitories.)
🍽 Special diets.
🚆 Midgham Station 1 mile away - walk or take taxi.
Focus
Christian/Catholic

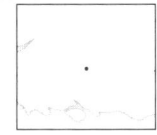

South East England/Berkshire

Emerson College

🕸 http://www.emerson.org.uk

Ian Lawton
Emerson College, Forest Row
RH18 5JX
✆ 01342 822238
📠 01342 826055
✉ mail@emerson.org.uk
✔ **Own Course Programme**
🛏 62 bedspaces (60 singles, 2 twins.)
🍽 Much of the food served at the college is made with biodynamic organic produce from neighbouring farms and from the market garden that is operated by students of the biodynamic agriculture training course. Special diets are always catered for.
🚆 East Grinstead by train, then bus 291/100 from Gatwick to Crawley, then bus 291. Alight at stop just after college driveway. Walk ½ mile up drive.

Emerson College was founded in 1962 and is a centre for adult education, training and research, all of which is based on Anthroposphy, the work of Rudolf Steiner (1861-1925). Anthroposophy investigates the whole interplay of the physical, the psychological and the spiritual in human life, and has a wide sphere of influence in many different fields of endeavour. Students are encouraged to develop their own insights and creative work without relying on dogmatic teachings of one kind or another.

Each year people from about 30 different countries, aged 18-80+, come here with th aim of finding ways of putting their ideals into practice, in education, the arts, agriculture and language. The common goal of finding a new impulse to take into the world gives urgency to the studies here, which take place in an atmosphere of an international community and a rich cultural life.

Course Programme

Emerson College is a residential college set in 15 acres of beautiful grounds in Forest Row near Ashdown Forest, East Sussex. Each year their is an intake for full time courses in Waldorf Steiner Teacher Training, Foundation Studies in Anthroposphy, Visual Arts, Sculpture, Storytelling, Creative Writing, Puppetry and Biodynamic Agriculture. There is also a gap year Orientation programme for 18-21 year olds. Throughout the academic year their are weekend workshops and in the summer there are several week long courses in a variety of subjects. These include: biodynamics, creative writing and poetry, storytelling, nutrition, meditation, eurythmy, bread-making, biographical counselling, sculpture, puppetry and theatre.
Focus Rudolf Steiner / Anthroposophy

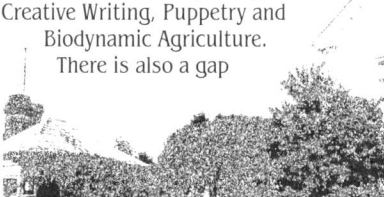

http://www.campionhouse.org

Osterley Retreats

Osterley is best known for the number of priests (over 1400) who started here. Now this same training has been extended to include men and women who do not seek ordination but who are preparing to take on positions of responsibility in the Church as the number of priests declines.

In addition it combines the training of priests with the work of a full-time Centre of Ignatian Spirituality. Our retreats are based on the Spiritual Exercises of St Ignatius Loyola, which help individuals to find the ways of praying that suit them best. Sometimes people use such a retreat to discern what way God is calling them, perhaps making a decision about a career or change of job, about religious life or marriage. But this is not always so; it is essentially a period of prayer. For all of us our vocation is seeking the next step along the path the Lord is leading us.

Event Types
Guided group retreats, guided individual retreats.

Subject Specialities
Arts & crafts, inner process, meditation, prayer, self expression, group process.

Suitability or Specialism
Adults.

Please note, we will be closing in August 2004.

Sr Annie Bromham
112 Thornbury Road
Osterley
Isleworth
Middlesex
TW7 4NN

✆ 020 8568 3821
✆ 020 8847 6227
osterley.retreats@btinternet.com

✔ **Retreat House**
✔ **Venue for hire**
group full board (up to £35), large indoor space, several small spaces
75 bedspaces (all singles)
Special diets.
Within walking distance of Osterley Underground Station (Piccadilly Line) and Isleworth railway station.

Focus
Christian

South East England/Greater London

Park Place Pastoral Centre

http://www.parkplacepastoralcentre.co.uk

Sister M Juliette FSMA
Park Place
Wickham
Fareham
Hampshire
PO17 5HA
✆ 01329 833043
✆ 01329 832226
✉ parkplacecentre@aol.com

✔ **Retreat House**
✔ **Own Course Programme**
✔ **Venue for hire**

🛏 60 beds, in 47 rooms, (28 rooms en-suite). A separate, self contained Youth Wing, catering for 25 young people plus 5 leaders, is also available.

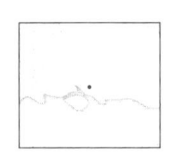

Focus All faith communities and lay groups

The Pastoral Centre is a unique and attractive location run by the Franciscan Sisters of St Mary of the Angels, situated near Wickham, a charming Hampshire village midway between Southampton, Portsmouth & Winchester. It offers a location where people of all Faiths, or none, can come together to develop their values helped by a temporary withdrawal from the purely material demands of every day life and relax in a peaceful and calm environment.
150 seater conference room, (with PA.) 3 smaller meeting rooms, a large dining room and a modern, simple chapel. All levels of catering from B & B to full board, for single days to full weeks. Simple vegetarian meals can be provided.
2 rooms on ground floor for disabled guests and carers.

ASSISI HOUSE, which can accommodate ten people in 2 twin bedded and 6 single bedded en-suite rooms, is a modern annexe to the Pastoral Centre. Assisi House offers an ideal facility for family, group or individual holidays, with many cultural, historic and religious attractions within a short bus or car drive. Groups and individuals are welcome to take meals in the Centre's dining room or prepare their own meals in the modern well-equipped kitchen.

Event Types
Organised retreats and days of recollection; Guests own retreats, meetings & courses; Holidays.

Subject Specialities
Sadhana Meditation & Yoga, painting and calligraphy, Indian cooking.

Redfield Centre

http://www.redfieldcommunity.org.uk

The Redfield Centre is a self-contained facility within the stable block adjacent to the Redfield Community, home to a group of up to 30 adults and children. The Centre has undergone extensive redevelopment and comprises of 3 bedrooms that sleep 4, a well-equipped kitchen, and a dining room. The extra accommodation is in 4 small dormitory-style bedrooms, each containing three or four beds. In the summer months, camping is an option for larger groups. The excellent vegetarian cuisine is renowned and special diets can be catered for. Self-catering groups also welcome. Seventeen acres of grounds, including woodland, organic gardens, orchard and tennis court.

Event Types
Own course programme, accredited courses.

Subject Specialities
Alternative lifestyles & technology.

Chrissie Schmidt
Redfield
Buckingham Road
Winslow
Buckingham
MK18 3LZ

✆ 01296 713661
✆ 01296 714983
✉ info@redfieldcommunity.org.uk

✔ **Own Course Programme**
✔ **Venue for hire**

⚲ 25 bedspaces.
🍽 Exclusively vegetarian, special diets.
🚆 Train to Aylesbury then Bus 66 to end of Redfield drive. Also some buses from Milton Keynes.

South East England/Buckinghamshire

Places to BE 2004/Page 105

Seekers Trust

http://www.theseekerstrust.org.uk

Ann Weller
The Close
Addington Park
West Malling
Kent
ME19 5BL

℅ 01732 843589
✆ 01732 842867
✉ theseekerstrust@supanet.com

✔ **Retreat House**
✔ **Venue for hire**
⇨ 5 single flats and 3 twin-bedded) flats.
♿ Limited wheelchair access at present but improvements planned.

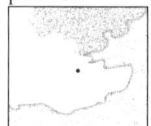

🚆 West Malling railway station, then 10 minute taxi ride.

Focus Non-denominational centre for prayer, absent and contact spiritual healing

For over 75 years, the Seekers Trust, set in 39 acres of parkland amid the beautiful Kent countryside, has been a centre for prayer and spiritual healing. A warm welcome awaits those who seek an informal retreat and/or spiritual healing. Through the harmony prayer circles thousands experiencing health, emotional and material problems have found help and gained new hope, thanks to our unique system of Christian prayer.

Accommodation
We have 5 single and 3 double (twin-bedded) self-catering flats. All with double glazing, central heating. Bed linen and towels are provided. We are open all year round.

Other facilities
Conference, workshop and seminar facilities also available with ample
car parking nearby.

Event Programme
Events are organised by out-side bodies. Diary available upon request.

Subject Specialities
Annual healing course run by Resident Trainer.

Suitability
Adults

Eco-tourism features
Set in 39 acres of parkland amid the beautiful Kent countryside, with our own woodland walks.

Woodrow High House

http://www.woodrow-high.co.uk

Woodrow High House is a historic listed building set in beautiful landscaped grounds and has a unique atmosphere. Woodrow's extensive facilities offer almost unlimited possibilities to visiting groups for their programme requirements. Residential bookings always represent good value providing shared accommodation for up to 53 visitors. There are large meeting rooms and lounge areas all furnished in a traditional style. The games room and arts and crafts rooms are popular venues for relaxation and learning.

Recreation, leisure and creative activities including the performing arts are well catered for in Woodrow's splendid new sports complex. There is a heated indoor swimming pool, showers, and changing rooms, a fully adaptable sports hall/auditorium with theatre stage plus recording and rehearsal rooms. Woodrow High House is owned and managed by The Federation of London Youth Clubs.

Event Types
Self directed retreats.

Subject Specialities
Outdoor activities & sport, arts & crafts.

Suitability or Specialism
Adults, families with children, women, men, young people 12 to 17, children under 12, older people.

Roy Hickman
Woodrow High House
Cherry Lane
Woodrow
Amersham
Buckinghamshire
HP7 0QG

☏ 01494 433531
✆ 01494 431391
✉ linda.collins@woodrow-high.co.uk

✓ **Retreat House**
✓ **Venue for hire**

🛏 53 bedspaces (1 single, 13 twins, 7 family rooms.)
🍽 Special diets.
♿ Wheelchair access.
🚆 Train to Amersham then taxi to Woodrow High House.

Other Places and Organisations

Benedictine Study & Arts Centre
74 Castlebar Road
Ealing
London
W5 2DD
Own Course Programme

Brahma Kumaris World Spiritual University
Global Co-operation House
65 Pound Lane
London
NW10 2HH
Own Course Programme

Burrswood
Groombridge
Tunbridge Wells
Kent
TN3 9PY

Centrespace
3 Alcroft Grange
Tyler Hill
Canterbury
Kent
CT2 9NN
Retreat House
✆ 01227 462038

Claridge House Healing Centre
Dormansland
Lingfield
Surrey
RH7 6QH
Retreat House

Eden Centre
252 Kingston Road
Teddington
Middlesex
TW11 9JQ
Retreat House

The Emmaus Centre
Layhams Road
West Wickham
Kent
BR4 9QJ
Venue for Hire

Four Winds Centre
High Thicket Road
Dockenfield
Farnham
Surrey
GU10 4HE
Venue for Hire

The Friars
Aylesford Priory
Aylesford
Kent
ME20 7BX
Venue for Hire

Global Retreat Centre
Nuneham Park
Nuneham Courtney
Oxford
OX44 9PG
Own Course Programme

Other Places and Organisations

The Grail Centre
125 Waxwell Lane
Pinner
Middlesex
HA5 3ER
Retreat House
© 020 8866 2195

The Haven
St Boniface Road
Ventnor
Isle of Wight
PO38 1PL
Retreat House

Hoffman Institute UK
Old Post House
Burpham
Arundel
West Sussex
BN18 9RH
Own Course Programme

Hourne Farm
Steel Cross
Crowborough
East Sussex
TN6 2SQ
Venue for Hire

Marie Reparatrice
115 Ridgway
Wimbledon
London
SW19 4RB
Retreat House

Marsh Farm Centre and Retreat
Binsted
Arundel
West Sussex
BN18 0LH
Own Course Programme

Centre of New Directions
White Lodge
Stockland Green Road
Speldhurst
Tunbridge Wells
Kent
TN3 0TT
Retreat House

Priory of Our Lady of Good Counsel
Sayers Common
Hassocks
West Sussex
BN6 9HT
Retreat House

Oxon Hoath
Hadlow
Tonbridge
Kent
TN11 9SS
Venue for Hire

Other Places and Organisations

Ruth White Yoga Centre
Church Farm House
Springclose Lane
Cheam
Surrey
SM3 8PU
Own Course Programme

St Columba's House
Maybury Hill
Woking
Surrey
GU22 8AB
Retreat House

St Ethelwold's
30 East St Helen's Street
Abingdon
Oxfordshire
OX14 5EB
Retreat House

Stacklands Retreat House
School Lane
West Kingsdown
Sevenoaks
Kent
TN15 6AN
Retreat House

Tekels Park Guest House
Tekels Park Estate
Camberley
Surrey
GU15 2LF

Bed & Breakfast
© 01276 23159
ghouse.tekels@btclick.com
http://www.tekelspark.co.uk

Worth Abbey Centre for Spirituality
Turners Hill
Crawley
West Sussex
RH10 4SB
Retreat House

Venues outside the UK

Venues in
France
Greece
India
Ireland
Italy
Portugal
Spain
Sri Lanka
Turkey

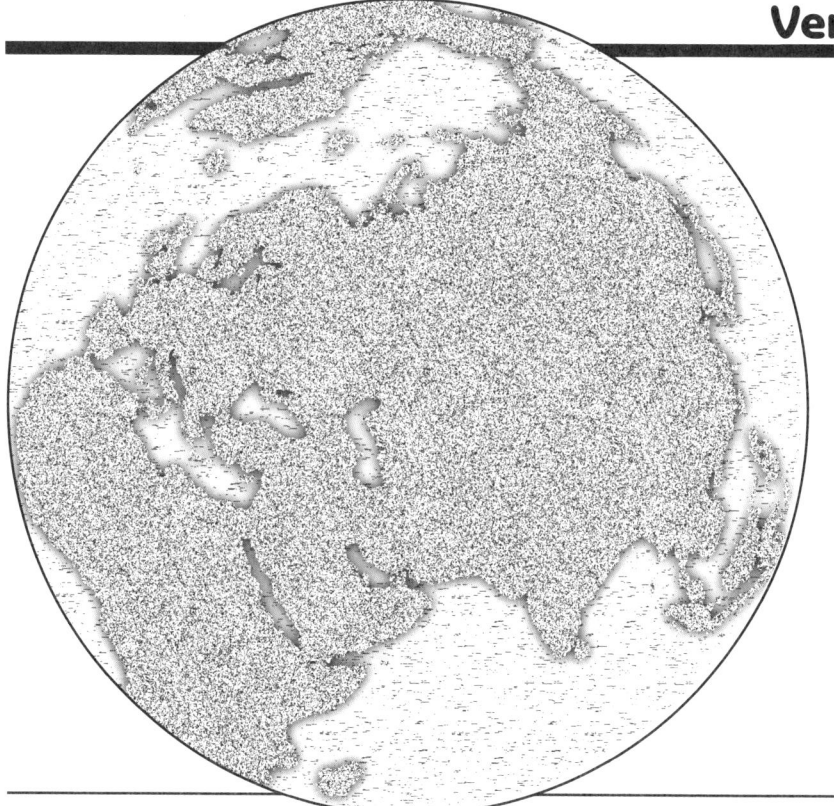

Places to BE

Le Blé en Herbe

Maria Sperring
Le Blé en Herbe
Puissetier
La Cellette
F-23350
France
© 0033 5 55806283
☏ 0033 5 55806283
✉ maria.sperring@gofornet.com

✔ **Bed & Breakfast**
✔ **Own Course Programme**
✔ **Venue for hire**

↝ 17 bedspaces (3 singles, 4 twins, 6 doubles.)
🍴 Exclusively vegetarian, special diets.
🚆 Train from Paris to Chateauroux. or bus from London to Limoges then train to Gueret. Collection by arrangement.

Focus Eco-spirituality

Le Blé en Herbe is a small, international holistic retreat with 7.5 acres of beautiful organic gardens, fields, woods, a large converted barn and farm guesthouse. Le Blé is located in central France in the gently rolling foothills of the Massif Central, a haven for wild flowers, butterflies and birds of prey. Visitors are offered a variety of refreshing holiday options in a nurturing, nourishing atmosphere. Delicious vegetarian/vegan meals are prepared with organic produce fresh daily from the "Sun" Garden. Produce for sale to self-catering guests. We offer B&B, full board, self-catering "Rose Cottage" (sleeps 2-4 people), camping and courses (herbalism, massage, dance, pottery). Nearest station is Gueret. Caen, Dieppe and Le Havre are 300 miles. Bookings only, maximum number of guests is 20.

Event Types
Guided group retreats, own course programme, working holidays.

Subject Specialities
Food & gardening, alternative lifestyles & technology, health & healing, arts & crafts, inner process, group process, earth mysteries.

Suitability or Specialism
Adults.

Eco-tourism features
Permaculture, solar and wind power (small scale), living willow structures.

http://www.lamaisonverte.co.uk

La Maison Verte

A 19th century wine grower's mansion in the Languedoc region of the South of France, available to group organisers for running courses, seminars, conferences and rehearsals. This private house belongs to sculptor Teddy Hutton and his wife Nicola Russell.

The Main House Sleeps up to 21 people and includes a vast drawing room, a television room, a large dining room, thirteen spacious and beautifully decorated bedrooms (four en-suite), kitchens, a pottery and an exhibition room.

It has a beautiful two acre garden with a large private pool, parking and small vineyard.

Workspaces The conference room, (160sq metres) and the wine barn for extra workshop space or as a refectory (100 sq metres). The pottery and the gallery are also available for exhibiting works.

Catering options: Organisers can choose to self-cater or to opt for full or half-board with the excellent range of local chefs and caterers.

Plus: four self-catering apartments for between two and five people all within the grounds. Regular visitors include the Cheltenham Festival of Literature, Il Collegio painting holidays, the Mediterranean Jazz Summer School and Free Spirit Travel, organisers of yoga, wine tasting and cookery holidays.

Nicola Russell
31 Avenue Henri Mas
Roujan
F-34320
France

✆ 0033 4672 48852
✆ 0033 4672 46998
✉ nicole.russell@wanadoo.fr

✔ **Holiday Operator**
✔ **Venue for hire**
group full board (£37.86 to £42.86), group self catering (£21.43 to £28.57)

♿ Courtyard apartment open plan, ground floor, specially designed and a separate unit entirely.

Outside the UK/France

Gaia Visions Retreat Zakynthos

http://www.gaiavisions.co.uk

Frances Engelhardt
36 Woodstock Avenue
Sutton
Surrey
SM3 9EF

© 020 8401 8319
gaiavisions@yahoo.com

✓ **Retreat House**
✓ **Holiday Operator**

12 bedspaces (4 twins, 2 doubles.)
Exclusively vegetarian.
Flight direct to Zakynthos, pick-up included in price. Alternatively bus and local flight connections from Athens – travel assistance given.
Focus Eco-spirituality

Located in the beautiful pristine peninsula of Vassilicos, Gaia Visions Retreat is a cultural and self-development centre. It is a place where you can learn and experience the real Greece, as well as have fun, take time for yourself and reconnect with nature and your own inner beauty.
We offer morning yoga and meditation, massage, nature walks and excursions plus the opportunity to take Greek dancing and/or self development courses. We can also organise horse-riding, ceramic-making, para-gliding, water-sports and mosaics. Accommodation is situated near to the beautiful beach of Gerakas – where the rare species of Loggerhead Turtle, the Caretta-Caretta, comes to rest. Participants are welcome to share and contribute in the running of this small, friendly community retreat. Accommodation is on a shared room basis unless otherwise requested. We specialise in offering all-inclusive programmes starting from £375 per person per week.

Event Types
Guided group retreats, guided individual retreats, business retreats.

Subject Specialities
Yoga, meditation, self development, health & healing, body & breathwork, self expression, outdoor activities & sport, counselling.

Suitability or Specialism
Adults, couples, lesbian women, gay men, women, men, older people.

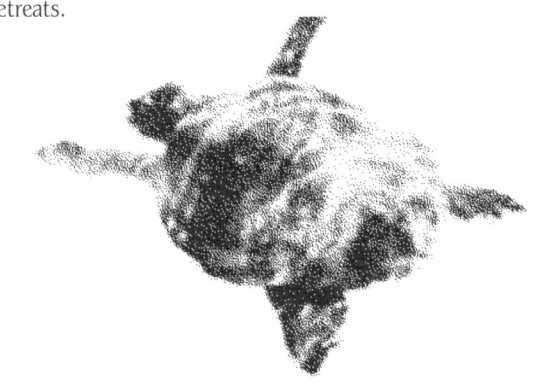

🖳 http://www.galiniholidays.co.uk

Galini Holidays

Galini in Greek means "tranquillity, serenity, calm" and we hope this is what you will find with us. Situated in the Peloponnese, mainland Greece, our house has stunning views over the ocean to the Taiyetos mountains and inland to peaceful vistas of hills and olive groves. We are a self-sufficient household, harnessing the power of sun and wind to generate our electricity and we have our own well for fresh water.

Accommodation
Large lounge/workshop room. Child friendly. No smoking in building. Open all year, with underfloor heating and open fires for the winter time.

Courses
These are run for small groups (max. 10), including yoga, reiki, menopause, solstice retreats, walking, wild flower weeks and Greek vegetarian cookery. Full board from £250 per week.

Tranquil Holidays
Where you are free to do as much or as little as you like. The sandy beach is only 25 minutes walk, there is quiet space to write or paint, take local walks through the olive groves, venture further afield to visit some of the ancient sites of the region ... or just sit on the terrace sipping chilled wine. Private treatments are available on all weeks. We also have working weeks.

Linda Vincent
Box 6064
Koroni
Messinias
G-24004
Greece
✆ 0030 6947 887342
✉ info@GaliniHolidays.co.uk
✔ **Retreat House**
✔ **Holiday Operator**
✔ **Own Course Programme**
✔ **Venue for hire**
🛏 8 bedspaces (4 twin rooms). Camping space. B&B, half or full board, from £110 per week.
🍽 Exclusively vegetarian – as much as possible our own home-grown organic produce. Special diets.
♿ Not suitable for wheelchair users
🚍 May to Oct: Fly to Kalamata. Nov to Apr: Fly to Athens, bus to Kalamata. We collect from Kalamata

Outside the UK/Greece

Spirit of Life Centre

http://www.thespiritoflife.co.uk

Sky Wickenden & Kerry Kousiounis
Henleaze Centre
13 Harbury Road
Henleaze
Bristol
BS9 4PN

✆ 0870 242 7069
✉ info@thespiritoflife.co.uk

✔ **Retreat House**
✔ **Holiday Operator**
✔ **Own Course Programme**
✔ **Venue for hire**

🛏 1 single, 2 twins, 2 doubles, 1 dormitory, further accommodation in village, camping.
🍽 Special diets.
♿ Wheelchair access difficult

The centre lies just above the fishing village of Agios Nicolaos. It is located in an area of outstanding natural beauty, with a backdrop of inspiring mountains and views over the blue Mediterranean. Less than a mile away is the larger village of Stoupa with its four beautiful sandy beaches and crystalline waters. It was built in the traditional Maniot style, using the stone crafted from the land itself. The Spirit of Life centre is located in the area that was ancient Lefkotron. Pausanias the 2nd Century Greek travel writer, recorded that there was a temple dedicated to Asclepius, the god of healing, in this area. It was at these healing temples that Therapeutes (the first therapists) used a mind, body and spirit approach to health and healing.

There is much to do (or not to do) in the locality with beautiful beaches, stunning walks and many optional classical tours (Ancient Messini, Gythion, Olympia, Mystras, and Kardamyli).This is perfect if you are also bringing a non-participating partner.

The food in the Peloponnese is excellent with many vegetarian choices and locally caught fresh fish. Our class numbers are small, up to 14 people for most classes. Our teachers are all very experienced and passionate about their subject. We are sure that you will be energised and inspired by the beauty and special heart energy of the area. If you wish you can enjoy optional healing sessions during your stay.

The course room is the entire upper floor of the centre building, with windows on every side providing wonderful views. A smooth woodern floor and many different lighting settings. It was purpose built for holding holistic courses. A large balcony is attached to the course room and there is also a covered pergola that is sometimes used for outside sessions.

The centre and facilities are also available for hire for spiritual / holistic training and group retreats. Please contact us for further details. We also run Dream Healing Pilgrimages in Greece, Turkey and Cyprus.

White Mountain Retreat

http://whitemountain-retreat.com

Much of what is available here in Crete at White Mountain Retreat is simple and God-given. Yet in this world where spin, speed and stress can make even the hardiest soul dizzy, maybe we can grasp this opportunity of quiet and space to breathe, enjoy and just Be. In offering simple retreat holidays and a selection of inspiring courses we consider your time with us to be precious. Our aim is to nourish and support your enjoyment in mind body and spirit.

We have a superb coastal situation surrounded by olive groves enjoying breathtaking views of sea, sky and mountains with a wonderful presence of healing energy.

A Time to Learn, A Time to Experience. A Time to Be Who You Really Are. Send for our Brochure for more details.

Event Types
Self directed retreats, own course programme, working holidays.

Subject Specialities
Health & healing, body & breathwork, inner process, meditation, self expression, yoga, earth mysteries, food & gardening, alternative lifestyles & technology, group process, outdoor activities & sport, arts & crafts.

Suitability or Specialism
Adults(++), couples, families with children, women, men, young people 12 to 17, older people.

Eco-tourism features
Organic farming and gardening; working to permaculture; solar panels.

Julie Murray Franks
25 Roman Road
Hove
East Sussex
BN3 4LB

✆ 01273 416050
✉ palamidi@aol.com
✔ **Retreat House**
✔ **Holiday Operator**
✔ **Own Course Programme**
✔ **Venue for hire**
group full board (£35 to £60), large indoor space, several small spaces

⌕ 20 bedspaces (2 singles, 5 twins, 2 doubles, 1 family room.)
🍽 Special diets.
🚍 Flights to Chania airport then 45 min by WMR car. Flights to Heraklion then taxi 2 hours or bus by day 3 hours.
Focus Eco-spirituality

Skyros Holistic Holidays

http://www.skyros.com

92 Prince of Wales Road
London
NW5 3NE

℡ 020 7284 3065
📠 020 7284 3063
✉ connect@skyros.com

✓ **Retreat House**
✓ **Holiday Operator**
✓ **Own Course Programme**

🍽 Special diets.

Holidays for the mind, the body and the spirit on the beautiful Greek island of Skyros and the exotic Thai island of Ko Samet. Established for 25 years as the foremost European 'alternative' holiday centre we offer two week sessions ranging from art, creative writing, personal development, T'ai Chi, yoga, healing and massage to singing, drumming, dance, laughter, mime and windsurfing. We also specialise in group therapy with world renowned therapists and writers' workshops with famous writers such as Sue Townsend, Margaret Drabble, Mavis Cheek, D M Thomas and many others. We offer delicious food and also cater for vegetarians. Our friendly community is situated in the most beautiful surroundings of the pine forest and sea of Atsitsa, the Skyros village and monastery of the Skyros Centre, and the rain forest and white squeaky beaches of Ko Samet. Prices (excluding travel) range from £450 to £945 for two weeks.

Subject Specialities
Alternative lifestyles & technology, arts & crafts, body & breathwork, conservation work, counselling, food & gardening, group process, health & healing, inner process, meditation, outdoor activities & sport, self expression.

Event Types
Self directed retreats, own course programme, accredited courses, working holidays.

Suitability
Adults, families with children, young people 12 to 17, children under 12, older people.

Outside the UK/Greece (Skyros)

http://www.beachandlakeresort.com

Beach and Lake Ayurvedic Resort

The Beach & Lake is a small (eight-roomed) privately owned Ayurvedic Resort, 8 km south of Trivandrum International Airport. It's nestled between the Arabian Sea and a river, situated on an island and blessed by nature. Access to the resort is only by private boat. Relax and receive the full benefit that such proximity to nature provides. All the bedrooms have verandas with a beach and lake view.

Ayurveda
Ayurveda is a health science, one of the oldest and most complete healing systems known. The word Ayurveda, derived from 2 Sanskrit terms, literally means the knowledge of life. At the heart of Ayurveda lies the concept of three 'doshas': Kapha, Pitha and Vatha. Balancing the three harmoniously will promote a healthy body and mind. This holistic treatment system involves various types of massage and oil applications, inhalations, diet, and natural medicines as required.

Ayurveda Package
(£270 per week)
Chose from a number of treatment programmes, including slimming, purification (detox), rejuvenation, and stress management with yoga. The inclusive package is for consultation and a daily treatment, plus full board and accommodation in twin rooms.

Private Hire
The resort is also available for private hire and would suit groups of 14 or less. There are various outdoor spaces suitable for yoga, t'ai chi, and art or dance type work shops.
Per day: £200 (min 1 week)
Full Board @ £5.00 per person
Tours, cultural entertainment evenings and Ayurvedic massage can be arranged as required.

Eco-tourism features
Resort blends with local nature. All staff are local.

Anil Elayath
Pozhikkara Beach
Pachalloor PO
Trivandrum
Kerala 27
India
© 0091 471 2382086
✆ 0091 471 2382066
✉ beach@
beachandlakeresort.com

✔ **Retreat House**
✔ **Holiday Operator**
✔ **Own Course Programme**
✔ **Venue for hire**

⌕ 16 bedspaces (8 twin rooms).
🍽 Special diets catered for.
🚆 Trivandrum Airport then 20 minute taxi transfer provided

Focus Ayurveda

Shanti Bhavan

http://www.shantibhavanyoga.com

Karen Sivan
Shanti Bhavan, Silent Valley
Kovalam, Vizhinjam PO
Trivandrum, Kerala 695521
India

✉ shantibhavanyoga@hotmail.com
- ✔ **Bed & Breakfast**
- ✔ **Holiday Operator**
- ✔ **Own Course Programme**
- 2 twin rooms
- No wheelchair access
- Trivandrum Airport then 16km taxi journey to Kovalam

Focus Yoga

Kovalam, a beach resort in Kerala, is a perfect place in which to 'live yoga' by practising the 5 main principles of Hatha Yoga, ie exercise (asanas) breath (pranyama) relaxation (rest) diet (vegetarian) and thought (positive thinking) on a daily basis.

Yoga
Shanti Bhavan is primarily a yoga centre with classes twice daily, led mostly by Sivan, who is from Kerala and teaches traditional Sivananda (Hatha) yoga. His courses are suitable for all levels of experience and are offered in weekly 6 or 12 class blocks. You can 'live yoga' under his guidance in an idyllic setting. Weekly courses: £25 / £45

Massage
Shanti Bhavan is also a massage centre, run by Sivan's wife Karen. An experienced and qualified therapist, Karen trained in London with Robert Tisserand in 1993, and first came to Kovalam in 1997. Her aromatherapy massage enables you to experience true relaxation and is an excellent partner to yoga exercise. £21 for 3 treatments

Houseguests
Finally, Shanti Bhavan is a comfortable home with most modern facilities. There are two twin guest rooms available if you would like to experience a 'homestay' style holiday, with Karen and Sivan as your hosts. Your safety and comfort will be ensured, friendship, help and advice readily available.

Weekly price including yoga and a massage: £145 sharing, £195 sole occupancy
Shanti Bhavan Booking Service: We provide help and advice on choosing alternative accommodation close to the centre, (from £1-£50 a night) reserve your room, and arrange for a taxi to collect you from the airport. £30
Main season: November-March. Discounts on accommodation during 'off season': June-October.

Eco-tourism features
Use local workforce and establishments as much as possible to generate income for local people. Support local people and projects by tithing percentage of project.

Chrysalis Holistic Centre

http://www.chrysalis.ie

Restful rural setting in Ireland (one hour south of Dublin) for homely holistic centre, specialising in residential workshops in many aspects of personal growth and spirituality, with facilities for private group bookings. Converted 18th century rectory and wooden chalet plus two delightful, comfortable octagonal hermitages situated in silent Zen meditation garden, both available for private retreats. Sauna, craft shop, organic garden, delicious meals, firm mattresses and a friendly red setter dog! We produce a biannual varied programme of events, available on request and we look forward to welcoming you to Ireland.

Event Types
Self directed retreats, own course programme, regeneration programmes.

Subject

Specialities
Body & breathwork, counselling, group process, inner process, meditation.

Suitability or Specialism
Adults.

Claire Harrison
Chrysalis
Donard
County Wicklow
Ireland

✆ 00353 45 404713
✆ 00353 45 404713
✉ peace@chrysalis.ie

✔ **Retreat House**
✔ **Own Course Programme**
✔ **Venue for hire**

⚲ 20 bedspaces (3 singles.)
🍽 Exclusively vegetarian, special diets.

Focus Ecumenical

Outside the UK/Ireland

Cloona Health Centre

http://www.cloona.ie

Dhara Kelly
Cloona Health Centre
Westport
County Mayo
Ireland

✆ 00353 98 25251
info@cloona.ie

✔ **Retreat House**
✔ **Own Course Programme**

10 bedspaces (10 singles.)
Exclusively vegetarian.
No wheelchair access.
Knock Airport or train to Westport then taxi.

Focus Celtic

When Cloona first opened its doors in 1973 we launched the concept of Health Tourism in Ireland. Our courses, both five-day (Sunday to Friday) and three-day (Thursday to Sunday) are exclusively residential. This, together with a quiet, rural location, ensures full privacy for our guests to enjoy what is intrinsically an experience in relaxation, self-care and de-toxifying. An energising, holistic programme, it consists of daily yoga, walks, sauna and massage and is based on a light, cleansing diet of fruit and vegetables that accords with the principles of proper food-combining. We have our own natural spring water on tap and are committed to the use of organic and GM-free produce.
Cloona is situated three miles from Westport, beside Croagh Patrick and Clew Bay.
Detox courses: 5-day (Sunday to Friday) €495; 3-day (Thursday to Sunday) €315

Event Types
Guided individual retreats, own course programme, programmes for healing and recovery.

Subject Specialities
Health & healing.

Suitability
Adults.

http://www.shamanismireland.com

Dunderry Park Transpersonal Centre

The Centre is situated in the heart of historic County Meath, close to the ancient sacred sites of Tara, Newgrange and Loughcrew, 45 minutes from Dublin airport. It is surrounded by 25 acres of wooded parkland. The house is a 200 year old Georgian residence which has been completely restored. There is, at present, shared accommodation for 32. The workroom is 41x19ft. Food is quality vegetarian. The Centre is available for hire to groups (minimum 18) for days, weekends or longer, at a cost of €55 per person per day, food and accommodation included. For further information on hiring the Centre or for a brochure on courses, please write or phone.

Event Types
Own course programme.

Subject Specialities
Body & breathwork, ritual & shamanic, Holotropic breathwork, Dance.

Donogh O'Connell
Dunderry Park
Navan
County Meath
Ireland

☏ 00353 46 9074455
✆ 00353 46 9074455
✉ dunderry@online.ie

✓ **Retreat House**
✓ **Holiday Operator**
✓ **Own Course Programme**
✓ **Venue for hire**

⌨ 32 bedspaces (1 single, 3 twins, 1 double, 4 family rooms, 1 dormitory.)
🍽 Exclusively vegetarian. Special diets.
♿ Slide chair for stairs.
🚌 10 minute drive from bus services.

Focus Shamanism/Transpersonal

Outside the UK/Ireland

The Phoenix

🔗 http://www.kerryweb.ie/destination-kerry/castlemaine/phoenix.html

Lorna or William
The Phoenix
Shanahill East
Castlemaine
County Kerry
Ireland

✆ 00353 669 766284
✆ 00353 669 766284
✉ phoenixtyther@hotmail.com

✔ **Bed & Breakfast**
✔ **Own Course Programme**

⚲ 15-20 bedspaces including chalet which sleeps family of 2-6 and costs euro450/week.
🍽 Exclusively vegetarian, special diets.
♿ Wheelchair access.
🚌 Buses run past house in summer months.

Situated on the south side of the Dingle Peninsula (R561), the Phoenix is a restored farmhouse with two acres of organic garden. Backed by the beautiful Slieve Mish Mountains and facing Castlemaine Harbour, there is plenty of scope for hill-walking. We have en-suite family rooms, hostel camping and a beautiful chalet to offer.
There is an on site restaurant, serving organic vegetarian meals from breakfast to dinner time. We use our own home grown salads and herbs, plus a rich selection of locally produced foods, such as organic goats' feta and yoghurts. We cater for special diets.
The emphasis is on a relaxed family run atmosphere. We are child friendly and pet friendly. See our website. B&B price euro35/person shared, 50% single supplement.

Event Types
Own course programme.
Subject Specialities
Meditation, inner process, alternative lifestyles & technology, food & gardening, outdoor activities & sport, conservation work, health & healing, body & breathwork, self expression.

Eco-tourism features
We work 2 acres of organic garden and use reedbed sewage.

http://www.sunflowerretreats.com

Sunflower Retreat Holidays

Experience an alternative holiday for the mind, body and soul in the beautiful hill top village of Casperia in Central Italy. Casperia lies in the heart of the Sabina Mountains and is quite unique as it is totally pedestrian, free from car fumes and pollution. Casperia is a place of natural beauty surrounded by olive groves, vineyards and forest covered mountains an ideal location to just BE!
Location is very convenient with easy access to Rome 1 hour, and Rome Airport 1 hour 30 minutes by bus and train running frequently from Casperia.
The holiday will be a real break in which to unwind, relax and physically and mentally recharge.
You decide how to spend your time, you can choose to:
- Practice Yoga Daily
- Have a Treatment from a wide range of Holistic Therapies, which include Aromatherapy and La Stone.
- Visit the Thermal Baths and Wild Hot Springs,
- Horse Ride through beautiful countryside.
- Take a Mountain or Country Walk
- Ski (available December to March)
- Cycle (Free use of our range of bicycles including our tandem)
- Swim (in wild mountain streams, and fresh mountain water swimming pools)
- Join an Excursion to Orvieto, St Francis Hermitages, Assisi etc...
Prices range from £275 To £395 including accommodation, breakfast, daily yoga class, free use of bikes, one guided walk.

Also new retreat Holiday starting in Talamone on the Tuscany coast 2004: for more info www.sunflowerretreats.com prices range from £495 per week.

Event types
Retreat Holidays, B&B, suitable for group leaders & teachers with own groups, Holistic breaks, Yoga Holidays, arts & crafts, body & breathwork, health & healing, meditation, outdoor activities & sport, relaxation

Lucy Bremner
Via Tito Tazo N° 11
Casperia, CAP
I-02041
Italy
✆ 0116 259 9422
✆ 0116 259 9422
✉ sunflowerretreats@tiscalinet.it
✔ **Holiday Operator**
✔ **Own Course Programme**
⌂ 15 bedspaces (4 singles, 7 twins, 7 double, 5 en suites, 2 family suites). In traditional village houses, or in the Casa Latini, a beautiful restored 13th century medieval house.
🚆 Train from Fiumicino Airport (Rome) to Poggio Mirteto, or to Orte via Poggio Mirteto. Local train station is Casperia; also free bus service from Poggio Mirteto to Casperia. We can collect you from station.
Focus Yoga

Moinhos Velhos

🔗 http://www.moinhos-velhos.com

Frank Jensen
Moinhos Velhos
Cotifo
Lagos
P-8600
Portugal

☏ 00351 282 687 147
📠 00351 282 687 697
✉ fasting@ip.pt

✔ **Holiday Operator**
✔ **Own Course Programme**

🛏 12 bedspaces (4 singles, 4 twins).
🍽 Exclusively vegetarian.

Focus New Age

Moinhos Veihos is a beautiful valley on the Algarve coast in Portugal. Inspired by the work of Drs Gerson and Bernard Jensen we offer the ultimate detoxification, purification and intestinal cleansing fasting program with juices and herbs. Transformation on the physical level is not our sole aim, but also on the emotional, mental and spiritual level. Thus we include yoga, meditation, therapeutic massage, Kinesiology and Bioresonans therapy as well as elimination of heavy metals and ACTS (the Automatic Computerised Treatments System). When we are not conducting a fasting program the facilities and services at Moinhos Velhos are available for other groups.

Event Types
Own course programme.

Subject Specialities
Health & healing.

http://www.cortijo-romero.co.uk

Cortijo Romero

Year round alternative holidays in Spain.

Deep in the South of Spain, in a magnificent setting between the mountains and the sea, is Cortijo Romero, a jewelled oasis ...

A stunningly beautiful, unspoilt environment; mountains, rivers, ancient hill villages and the nearby fabled city of Granada. Delightful buildings in a typical Andalucian style, with beautiful gardens and orchards, set in an 800-year old olive grove. A superb pool surrounded by masses of flowers throughout the year, palm trees, and shaded courtyards. Comfortable rooms, all with bath or shower. Delicious food, with a wide variety of local produce.

A warm and supportive atmosphere, with a devoted and knowledgeable Anglo-Spanish staff.

The best climate in Europe, with 315 days of sunshine per year. Average temperatures are 7-10°C (15-18°F) above London, the humidity is low and the annual rainfall a mere 15in.

Holiday Courses in Personal Development include Alexander Technique, The Authentic Self, Bodywork, Serious Fun, Creative Expression, Dance and Music, Embodying the Spirit, Getting Out Of Your Own Way, The Inner Journal, Massage and Inspiration, Flamenco Dance, Living With Heart And Soul, The Challenge to Be Alive, T'ai Chi, Voice and Movement, Yoga and lots more ...

Plus optional sessions of expressive dance, flamenco, structured counselling, massage, reflexology, shiatsu, Thai yoga ...

Not to mention lazing by the pool, good company, excursions to ancient villages and wild countryside.

Development, Community, Celebration!

Subject Specialities
Body & breathwork, inner process, meditation, self expression, group process, ritual & shamanic, counselling, local culture, self-development, voice & dance.

Suitability or Specialism
Adults.

Janice Gray
Cortijo Romero
22 Cottage Offices
Latimer Park, Latimer
Chesham HP5 1TU

© 01494 765775
℡ 01494 766577
✉ bookings@cortijo-romero.co.uk

✔ **Retreat House**
✔ **Holiday Operator**
✔ **Own Course Programme**
✔ **Venue for hire**

group full board (£25 to £50), large indoor space, several small spaces

⌘ 10 singles, 7 twins, 2 doubles and 2 apartments.

🍽 Exclusively vegetarian, special diets.

♿ Terraced site but wheelchair access to most parts.

✈ Málaga then 2 hours by minibus.

Argayall: Place of Light

🌐 http://www.argayall.com

Sadyana
Argayall
Valle Gran Rey
La Gomera
E-38870
Canary Islands

✆ 0034 922 697008
✆ 0034 922 805551
✉ info@argayall.com

✔ **Own Course Programme**
🛏 29 bedspaces (2 singles, 13 doubles.)
🍴 Exclusively vegetarian.
🚌 Flight to Tenerife Sur, ferry to La Gomera, taxi or bus to Valle Gran Rey.

Focus holistic

On the Canarian island La Gomera, following the stony road behind the harbour of Valle Gran Rey, you'll find our Finca Argayall. Situated in its own bay, embedded between the ocean and the mountains this is a unique place of stunning beauty and intense energy.

An international community of around 20 people is living and working together here and offers space for individuals as well as for groups to combine holiday and healing, relaxation and self-experience, celebration and ...

Event Types
Guided group retreats, business retreats, own course programme, regeneration programmes.

Subject Specialities
Health & healing, alternative lifestyles & technology, group process, inner process, body & breathwork, self expression, meditation, food & gardening, permaculture, dolphins and whales.

Suitability or Specialism
Adults.

Places to BE 2004/Page 128

Outside the UK/Spain (Canary Islands)

Yuva

🌐 http://www.vegiventures.com

Eco Holiday Village: peaceful mountain location, secluded cove for swimming and snorkelling, great vegetarian/vegan food. Centre available for hire.

Yuva is a holiday/retreat centre in south-west Turkey, on 40 acres of protected forest, an area of outstanding natural beauty, in the mountains, right by the sea. Local farmers cultivate ancient terraces, growing grains, fruit and olives. This is the perfect place to relax and enjoy a healthy holiday. Yuva, which means 'homestead' in old Turkish, is run by Atilla Sevilmis and his family, extending warm traditional Turkish hospitality. The main accommodation is in 4 buildings, constructed of natural materials. Each building has 2 spacious twin/double rooms, overlooking the bay. There are also 5 log cabins, suitable as single rooms. All rooms have electricity and ensuite shower and toilet. Some of the larger rooms can be comfortably used as triples. The food is delicious Turkish style vegetarian/vegan. Yuva is suitable for groups of up to 24 people. There is a purpose built group-work/yoga platform with breathtaking views. Yuva has excellent swimming from its rocky cove or take the local bus to the lagoon and beach at Ölüdeniz, about 25 minutes drive. Optional activities from Ölüdeniz include: scuba diving, paragliding, boat trips, archaeological excursions... The recently mapped 'Lycian Way', a long distance route, passes near to Yuva, making it ideal for walking and outdoor holidays/courses of all types. For groups of 10 or more, phone or email for details and special low rates. For individual/family holidays ask for VegiVentures holiday brochure.

Event Types
Guided group retreats, self directed retreats, business retreats, working holidays.

Suitability or Specialism
Adults, couples, women, men, young people 12 to 17.

Eco-tourism features
Organic home-grown food, where possible. Buildings are of natural materials. Solar hot water heating. Deep respect for local traditions.

Nigel Walker
Castle Cottage, Castle Acre
King's Lynn, Norfolk
PE32 2AJ

✆ 01760 755888
✉ yuva@vegiventures.com

✔ **Retreat House**
✔ **Bed & Breakfast**
✔ **Holiday Operator**
✔ **Venue for hire**
↳ 24 bedspaces (5 singles, 5 twins, 3 doubles, 3 family rooms.)
🍽 Exclusively vegetarian, special diets.

Outside the UK/Turkey

Other Places and Organisations

FRANCE

Agora Centre of Ayurvedic Medicine
Le Lac
Seignalens
F-11240
France
Holiday Venue

Beau Champ
Montpeyroux
Dordogne
F-24610
France
Community

Bellenau
Château Bel Enault
Saint-Côme-du-Mont
Carentan, Normandy
F-50500
France
Venue for Hire

Lavaldieu
Rennes-le-Château
F-11190
France
Own Course Programme

Le Plessis
Plumaudan
F-22350
France
Venue for Hire

Under the Lime Tree
Le Tilleul
Fontfaix le Haut
Cellefrouin
F-16260
France
Own Course Programme
info@underthelimetree.com

GREECE

Azogires
2 The Grove
London Road
Hartley Wintney
Hook
Hampshire
RG27 8RN
Holiday Venue

Other Places and Organisations

Peligoni Club
PO Box 88
Chichester
West Sussex
PO20 7DP
Holiday Venue

West Crete Holidays and Holistic Centre
The Old Olive Mill
Potamida 137
Kissamos
Crete
GR-73400
Greece
Holiday Venue

Yoga Plus
177 Ditchling Road
Brighton
East Sussex
BN1 6JB
Holiday Venue

Lios Dána Holistic Centre
Inch-Annascaul
County Kerry
Ireland
Retreat House

IRELAND

Green Lodge
Pearson's Bridge
Ballylickey
Bantry
County Cork
Ireland
Bed & Breakfast

Skyhil
Glengarrif
Bantry
County Cork
Ireland
Bed & Breakfast
✆ 00353 27 63610

PORTUGAL

A Colina Atlântica
Quinta das Maçãs
Travessa dos Melquites 3
Barrantes
Salir de Matos
P-2500-621
Portugal
Holiday Venue

Other Places and Organisations

SPAIN

El Bosque
C/ Del Guerrero 5
Mataelpino
Madrid
E-28492
Spain
Own Course Programme

Eco Forest
Apdo 29
Coín
29100
Málaga
Spain
Holiday Venue

✆ 0034 661 079 950
Harmonic Healing Foundation
Agüilla Ensalada
Apartado 32
Tabernas
Almeria
E-04200
Spain
Bed & Breakfast

SRI LANKA

Barberyn Ayurveda Resorts
Barberyn Reef Hotel
Beruwala
Sri Lanka
Holiday Venue

Ulpotha
Neal's Yard Agency
BCM Neal's Yard
London
WC1N 3XX
Holiday Venue

TURKEY

Health and Yoga Holidays
133a Devonshire Road
London
SE23 3LZ
Holiday Venue

Huzur Vadisi
12 Trinity Road
Aberystwyth
Ceredigion
SY23 1LU
Holiday Venue

Holiday and Tour Operators

Sandra Straw Spiritual Holidays

www.wellbeingretreats.com, www.spiritualholidays.com

Sandra Straw
112 Broadfield Estate
Broadhurst Gardens
London
NW6 3QR

℅ 020 7604 3628
info@circleoflight.co.uk

✓ **Holiday Operator**
✓ **Own Course Programme**

The Magic of being at One. Sandra Straw and her company Spiritual Holidays and Circle of Light was founded 15 years ago as a result of a near death experience in her life. Her journey into healing ensued. She has trained under people such as Louise Hay, Dr Deepak Chopra, Chuck Spezzano, Tony Robbins NLP. She is a metaphysical counsellor, healer and spiritual life coach and Reiki Master of the highly acclaimed Eastern lineage. She lectures extensively as well as working in the business world where she introduces her Wellbeing retreats which reduce stress, bring work/life balance, relationship issues, abundance and communication.

Her outer/inner journeys began after a visit to Mother Meera to whom she currently takes groups 3-4 times a year. Sandra helps people to explore their personal journey and the MAGIC OF BEING – that "Oneness" state, on her transformational journeys to places such as Timeless Tibet, Nepal and Spiritual India, following in the Buddha's footsteps, and to Dharamsala, John O'God, Sacred Peru, the Amazon, Ancient Egypt, Mind Body Spirit Nile Cruises, Lemeurian Hawaii, the Maya lands, Magical Sedona and New Mexico. She draws on her multifold experience of the ancient teachings of the planet and reaches beneath their individual forms of presentation to bring us the core teachings at a cellular level.

Whilst an overall proposed itinerary exists for each journey and pilgrimage, groups are small and intimate enough to allow for the teachings as well as giving each person free time. Accommodation can be 4 star or budget. Sandra honours the eco systems and culture wherever she goes often accompanied by Shamans, Mayan Elders and Hopi Indians. Sandra also hosts walking holidays in Devon, near her home, which give a more simplistic experience of her work.

Her recent focus is on her Wellbeing retreats held in various places in England for both businesses, and include stress release techniques, work/life balance, relationship healing which includes techniques such as meditation, Tai Chi or yoga, breathing methods, communication and healing. Sandra creates a space where you can have the opportunity to be inwardly still and reflective.

VegiVentures

http://www.vegiventures.com

VegiVentures provides holidays with great vegetarian/vegan food and "A touch of healthy living." Founded in 1989 by Swiss-trained chef and yoga teacher Nigel Walker, destinations now include holidays in Britain, Turkey and Peru. Some holidays are very laid back, eg Turkey, relax on the terrace enjoying the stunning sea and mountain views, stroll around ancient sites or chill-out on a secluded beach. The Lake District holidays invite you to breathe in lung-fulls of fresh mountain air while stretching your legs over England's most beautiful hills and valleys. Peru is more challenging, thrilling high altitude journeys into the land of the Incas. Prices range from a "Creativity Weekend" in the UK for £79, Christmas house-party on Exmoor from £229 for 4 nights, to 3 weeks in Peru for about £1290 (excluding flights). All holidays are ideal for men, women and couples. Phone or email for a free brochure.

Location
Europe including the UK, Middle East and North Africa, South America.

Types of Holiday
Small group, tailor made, working holidays, walking.

Subject Specialities
Local culture, ancient sites, arts & crafts, yoga, creativity, meditation.

Suitability or Specialism
Adults, couples, young people 12 to 17. People recovering from illness, average fitness levels.

Nigel Walker
Castle Cottage
Castle Acre
King's Lynn
Norfolk
PE32 2AJ

✆ 01760 755888
✉ holidays@vegiventures.com

✔ **Holiday Operator**
✔ **Own Course Programme**

🍽 Exclusively vegetarian.

Holidays in Britain, Turkey and Peru

Other Places and Organisations

Alternative Holidays UK
4 Alexandra Gardens
Ebury Road
Sherwood Rise
Nottingham
NG5 1BA
Holiday Operator

BAOBAB - Alternative Roots to Travel
Old Fallings Hall
Old Fallings Lane
Wolverhampton
WV10 8BL
Holiday Operator

Bicycle Beano
Erwood
Builth Wells
Powys
LD2 3PQ
Holiday Operator

Dance Holiday Company
Carefree Travel International Ltd
Zurich House
East Park
Crawley
West Sussex
RH10 6AJ
Holiday Operator

Dolphin Connection
Second Floor
46 Osmond Road
Hove
East Sussex
BN3 1TD
Holiday Operator

Dolphin Swims
PO Box 5872
Forres
Morayshire
IV36 1WA
Holiday Operator

Encounter
Camp Green
Debenham
Stowmarket
Suffolk
IP14 6LA
Holiday Operator

Exodus
9 Weir Road
London
SW12 0LT
Holiday Operator

Footprint Adventures
5 Malham Drive
Lincoln
LN6 0XD
Holiday Operator

Free Spirit Travel
153 Carden Avenue
Brighton
East Sussex
BN1 8LA
Alternative Travel Agent

Other Places and Organisations

Harmony Journeys
23 Severn Drive
Walton-on-Thames
Surrey
KT12 3BH
Holiday Operator

HF Holidays
Imperial House
Edgware Road
London
NW9 5AL
Holiday Operator

High Places
Globe Centre
Penistone Road
Sheffield
S6 3AE
Holiday Operator

KE Adventure Travel
32 Lake Road
Keswick
Cumbria
CA12 5DQ
Holiday Operator

Naturetrek
Cheriton Mill
Alresford
Hampshire
SO24 0NG
Holiday Operator

Neals Yard Agency
BCM Neals Yard
London
WC1N 3XX
✆ 0870 444 2702
✉ info@nealsyardagency.com
⚓ http://
www.nealsyardagency.com

Agents for:
Cortijo Romero *p127*
Peligoni Club *p131*
Barberyn *p132*
Ulpotha *p132*
Health and Yoga Holidays *p132*
Huzur Vadisi *p132*

Nepalese Trails
Random Cottage
Pentre
Llanfyllin
Powys
SY22 5LE
Holiday Operator

Palanquin Travels Ltd
Ray Powell Travel Ltd
42 High Street
Wanstead
E11 2RJ
Holiday Operator

Other Alternative Holiday and Tour Operators

Other Places and Organisations

Pure Portugal
✆ info@pureportugal.co.uk
⚓ http://
www.pureportugal.co.uk
Alternative Travel Agent

The Retreat Company
The Manor House
Kings Norton
Leicester
LE7 9BA
☏ 0116 259 9211
Alternative Travel Agent

SAcred Tours
DEO
249 Carr Road
Northolt
Middlesex
UB5 4RN
Holiday Operator

Sherpa Expeditions
131a Heston Road
Hounslow
Middlesex
TW5 0RD
Holiday Operator

Walks Worldwide
Kings Arms Building
15 Main Street
High Bentham
Lancaster
LA2 7LG
Holiday Operator

Wild Woman
62 Falkner Street
Liverpool
L8 7QA
Own Course Programme

Window to the World
44a Royar Thoppu
Srirangam
Trichy
Tamil Nadu
620006
India
Holiday Operator

World Expeditions
4 Northfields Prospect
Putney Bridge Road
London
SW18 1PE
Holiday Operator

World Spirit
12 Vale Road
Altrincham
Cheshire
WA14 3AQ
Holiday Operator

Bed & Breakfast Seeker's Index

The B&B Seeker's Index is fairly self-explanatory. The entries listed have all said that they offer bed and breakfast and/or full board to individuals. However, standards may vary enormously and will range from conventional (and often) salubrious tourist board recommended venues to very unconventional intentional communities that offer a B&B option to visitors as one way of giving a short-term taste of their lifestyle. So please phone ahead, not only to check on availability but also to make sure that you know exactly what you're going to.

Vegetarian means that the establishment say they are exclusively vegetarian; some of these will be exclusively vegan (see their full page entry) - and of course they may well cater for more restrictive **Special Diets** within that basic parameter.

No smoking usually means within buildings – there may sometimes be a special smoking room.

Children over 5 and **Children under 5** refer to the suitability of the venue to children in those age ranges. A very few places have said that they can offer a **Children Minding** service but don't expect this to be available on demand.

Whlchr Access indicates a level of accessibility to wheelchair users. Some places give more details of access in their full page listing.

Max B&B shows the maximum daily charge for B&B where this has been stated – please make allowances for changes over time.

page number	Venue	Individ B&B	Individ full board	Vegetarian	No Smoking	Special Diets	Children over 5	Children under 5	Child Minding	Whlchr Access	Max B&B
	Scotland										
12	Burgh Lodge	◆								◆	£10
15	Glengorm	◆									
	North of England										
24	Losand Dragpa	◆	◆	◆	◆	◆	◆	◆			
	East of England										
36	Marshwinds	◆	◆	◆	◆	◆					£70
	Midlands										
41	The Grange	◆			◆	◆	◆	◆		◆	£31
	Wales										
51	Coleg Trefeca	◆	◆		◆	◆	◆	◆		◆	
53	Cwmllechwedd	◆			◆	◆					£30
54	Heartspring	◆		◆			◆	◆			£40
55	Woodlands	◆			◆						£29
61	Trigonos	◆			◆	◆		◆		◆	£28.50
	South West England										
66	Ammerdown Centre	◆	◆		◆	◆	◆	◆		◆	£32.50
68	Beacon Centre			◆		◆	◆	◆			£18
69	Beech Hill	◆	◆		◆	◆	◆	◆		◆	£15

Places to BE 2004/Page 140   Bed & Breakfast Seeker's Index

page number	Venue	Individ B&B	Individ full board	Veget-arian	No Smoking	Special Diets	Children over 5	Children under 5	Child Minding	Whlchr Access	Max B&B
70	Boswednack Manor	◆		◆	◆	◆		◆			£23
75	Hawkwood	◆	◆		◆	◆				◆	
76	Hazelwood House	◆	◆			◆	◆	◆		◆	£37
79	Little Burrows	◆	◆	◆	◆	◆	◆	◆		◆	£29
80	Lower Shaw	◆	◆	◆	◆	◆	◆	◆	◆	◆	£15
82	Middle Piccadilly	◆	◆	◆	◆						£30
83	Monkton Wyld	◆	◆		◆	◆	◆	◆			£26
85	Samways	◆		◆		◆					
86	Sancreed House	◆		◆		◆					£25
88	Shambhala	◆		◆	◆	◆	◆				£35
90	Tordown	◆		◆	◆		◆	◆			£25
91	Trevina	◆	◆	◆	◆	◆					£23
	South East England										
97	The Abbey	◆	◆	◆	◆						£30
	Outside the UK										
112	Le Blé en Herbe	◆	◆	◆	◆	◆	◆				
120	Shanti Bhavan	◆			◆						
124	Phoenix	◆	◆	◆	◆	◆	◆	◆		◆	
129	Yuva	◆	◆	◆	◆	◆	◆				

Retreat Seeker's Index

This is the index for you if you're looking for a retreat. Of primary concern to you will probably be whether the venue adheres to a particular faith or has a specific spiritual orientation. For this reason the different places appear in the index grouped according to their spiritual focus. First there are the places that have no particular orientation or else have a focus with few representatives in the book. Eco-spiritual and New Age are popular modern orientations. Christian and Buddhist retreat houses respectively are grouped together but you may find more specific classifications on the venue's own page. **Group** means that they offer guided retreats for groups; **Individ** means guided retreats for individuals; **Self D** generally means that a supportive environment is provided for people who are directing their own retreats. **Business** means that a retreat environment can be offered to groups from commercial and voluntary organisations. **Progs** refers to the availability of programmes for healing and recovery to assist people who are coming out of some kind of crisis. **Medit** and **Prayer** means that instruction in meditation and prayer are amongst the specialities on offer. **Whlchr** indicates a level of wheelchair access; some organisations give more details in their full page entry.

page	Venue	Region	Group	Individ	Self D	Business	Progs	Medit	Prayer	Whlchr
16	Laurieston	Scotland			◆					◆
23	Brightflife	North of England	◆							◆
29	Orange Tree	North of England	◆	◆	◆	◆	◆			◆
37	Voewood	East of England	◆	◆	◆	◆				
50	Buckland Hall	Wales	◆			◆				◆
52	Cryndir	Wales			◆	◆				
54	Heartspring	Wales		◆	◆		◆			
55	Woodlands	Wales			◆					

page	Venue	Region	Group	Individ	Self D	Business	Progs	Medit	Prayer	Whlchr
57	Old Rectory	Wales			◆	◆		◆		
58	Pen Rhiw	Wales	◆							◆
60	Spirit Horse	Wales	◆							
61	Trigonos	Wales			◆					◆
75	Hawkwood	South West England	◆		◆	◆				◆
76	Hazelwood House	South West England	◆		◆	◆				◆
79	Little Burrows	South West England	◆	◆	◆					◆
81	Magdalen Project	South West England			◆	◆				◆
82	Middle Piccadilly	South West England		◆	◆	◆				
86	Sancreed House	South West England			◆		◆			
87	Self Realization	South West England	◆	◆	◆	◆	◆	◆		
90	Tordown	South West England	◆	◆	◆					
92	Wild Pear	South West England	◆		◆					
97	The Abbey	South East England	◆		◆	◆				
98	Braziers	South East England	◆	◆	◆	◆				
100	Commonwork	South East England			◆	◆				◆
107	Woodrow	South East England			◆					◆
115	Galini	Outside the UK	◆		◆			◆		
118	Skyros	Outside the UK			◆					
119	Beach and Lake	Outside the UK					◆			

page	Venue	Region	Group	Individ	Self D	Business	Progs	Medit	Prayer	Whlchr
122	Cloona	Outside the UK		◆			◆			
127	Cortijo Romero	Outside the UK	◆	◆		◆	◆			◆
129	Yuva	Outside the UK	◆		◆	◆				
Eco-Spiritual										
18	Shanti Griha	Scotland	◆	◆	◆					
48	Ancient Healing Ways	Wales	◆					◆	◆	◆
68	Beacon Centre	South West England	◆					◆		
71	EarthSpirit	South West England	◆							◆
89	Shekinashram	South West England	◆		◆			◆		
114	Gaia Visions	Outside the UK	◆	◆		◆				
117	White Mountain	Outside the UK			◆					
Christian										
26	Holy Rood House	North of England	◆	◆	◆	◆				◆
27	Lattendales	North of England			◆		◆			◆
30	Rookhow Centre	North of England	◆		◆	◆				
31	St Oswald's	North of England	◆	◆	◆				◆	◆
66	Ammerdown Centre	South West England	◆	◆	◆				◆	◆
84	St Peter's Grange	South West England	◆	◆	◆			◆		◆
99	Charney Manor	South East England	◆		◆	◆				◆
101	Douai Abbey	South East England	◆		◆	◆		◆		

page	Venue	Region	Group	Individ	Self D	Business	Progs	Medit	Prayer	Whlchr
103	Osterley	South East England	◆	◆						
104	Park Place	South East England	◆	◆	◆			◆		
106	Seekers Trust	South East England			◆					
121	Chrysalis	Outside the UK			◆		◆			
Buddhist										
24	Losang Dragpa	North of England	◆	◆	◆					
28	Manjushri	North of England	◆					◆		
67	The Barn	South West England	◆			◆	◆	◆		
70	Boswednack Manor	South West England	◆		◆		◆	◆		
73	Gaia House	South West England	◆	◆				◆		
77	Int Meditation Centre	South West England	◆					◆		
New Age										
17	Newbold	Scotland			◆					
49	Anglesey Healing	Wales	◆		◆			◆		
59	Rainbow Rose	Wales	◆	◆	◆					
88	Shambhala	South West England			◆					
116	Spirit of Life	Outside the UK	◆	◆		◆	◆			
123	Dunderry Park	Outside the UK	◆							◆

Retreat Seeker's Index

Workshop Seeker's Index

The types of places listed in this book are (quite rightly) very resistant to classification. However, for the book to be useful a degree of classification is necessary. The categories are meant to be starting points. Venues will describe what they offer in more detail in their written descriptions. The S-codes in this index are explained in the list alongside. Places will offer courses and workshops within these broad subject areas but not necessarily everything that is described.

S1 Arts & Crafts
drawing; painting; pottery; etc
S2 Self expression
music; writing; drama, etc
S3 Bodywork & Breathwork
yoga; t'ai chi; massage; bio-energetics; breathwork; rebirthing; etc
S4 Health & Healing
acupressure; aromatherapy; homeopathy; psychic healing; etc
S5 Outdoor activities & Sport
walking; climbing; inner sport; etc
S6 Conservation work
woodland work; hedge laying; etc
S7 Food & Gardening
diet modification; cookery; organic gardening; permaculture;
S8 Alternative lifestyles & technology
communal living; technology; etc
S9 Counselling
spiritual; psychotherapeutic; individuals; couples; etc
S10 Inner process
dreamwork; gestalt; hypnosis; regression; etc
S11 Group process
teamwork; trust building; psychodrama; etc
S12 Ritual & Shamanic
vision quest; ancient wisdom; ceremony; etc
S13 Earth mysteries
ancient sites; geomancy; etc
S14 Meditation
guided visualisation; attunement; inner listening; concentration; etc
S15 Prayer
contemplative; devotional; chanting; mantras; etc

work means that they can sometimes offer working holidays to people.

acc means that some of the courses on offer carry accreditation.

teach means that they run teacher training courses.

Workshop Seeker's Index

page	Venue	S1	S2	S3	S4	S5	S6	S7	S8	S9	S10	S11	S12	S13	S14	S15	work	acc	teach
	Scotland																		
11	Beshara														♦				
13	Isle of Erraid							♦							♦				
14	Findhorn	♦	♦		♦		♦	♦	♦		♦	♦			♦	♦		♦	
16	Laurieston		♦	♦			♦	♦	♦			♦					♦		
17	Newbold								♦						♦				
18	Shanti Griha	♦	♦	♦	♦	♦		♦	♦						♦				♦
	North of England																		
23	Brightlife				♦					♦					♦				
24	Losang Dragpa														♦	♦	♦		♦
26	Holy Rood House	♦	♦	♦	♦					♦	♦	♦			♦	♦		♦	
27	Lattendales			♦											♦	♦			
28	Manjushri														♦		♦		
29	Orange Tree			♦	♦	♦									♦				
31	St Oswald's															♦			
32	Swarthmoor Hall										♦	♦				♦			
	Midlands																		
41	The Grange	♦	♦	♦		♦					♦				♦	♦			
44	Woodbrooke	♦	♦		♦			♦			♦			♦	♦	♦	♦		

page	Venue	S1	S2	S3	S4	S5	S6	S7	S8	S9	S10	S11	S12	S13	S14	S15	work	acc	teach
	Wales																		
48	Ancient Healing Ways												◆	◆	◆	◆			
49	Anglesey Healing				◆						◆			◆	◆				
51	Coleg Trefeca	◆	◆												◆				
56	Life Foundation				◆														◆
58	Pen Rhiw	◆		◆		◆								◆	◆				
59	Rainbow Rose		◆		◆		◆	◆	◆	◆	◆	◆		◆	◆		◆		
60	Spirit Horse	◆	◆	◆	◆					◆	◆	◆	◆	◆	◆	◆			
61	Trigonos	◆		◆	◆			◆	◆	◆				◆					
	South West England																		
66	Ammerdown Centre	◆	◆	◆	◆						◆			◆	◆			◆	
67	The Barn							◆	◆			◆		◆			◆		
68	Beacon Centre	◆	◆	◆	◆						◆	◆		◆					
70	Boswednack Manor			◆									◆	◆					
73	Gaia House													◆					
74	Grimstone		◆	◆	◆			◆	◆		◆	◆	◆	◆			◆	◆	
75	Hawkwood	◆	◆	◆	◆				◆			◆	◆	◆	◆				
76	Hazelwood House				◆			◆	◆				◆						
77	Int Meditation Centre													◆					
79	Little Burrows	◆	◆	◆	◆			◆	◆	◆				◆					

page	Venue	S1	S2	S3	S4	S5	S6	S7	S8	S9	S10	S11	S12	S13	S14	S15	work	acc	teach
80	Lower Shaw	◆	◆					◆	◆								◆		
81	Magdalen Project					◆	◆	◆											
82	Middle Piccadilly				◆														
83	Monkton Wyld	◆		◆	◆		◆			◆	◆		◆		◆		◆		
85	Samways			◆		◆													
86	Sancreed House	◆	◆		◆					◆	◆				◆				
87	Self Realization		◆	◆	◆					◆	◆	◆			◆	◆		◆	◆
88	Shambhala			◆	◆					◆	◆				◆				
89	Shekinashram			◆	◆			◆		◆					◆				
90	Tordown				◆					◆									◆
91	Trevina						◆	◆	◆						◆				
	South East England																		
97	The Abbey		◆								◆	◆			◆				
98	Braziers	◆	◆	◆		◆	◆	◆	◆			◆	◆		◆		◆		
99	Charney Manor	◆	◆		◆						◆			◆	◆	◆			
100	Commonwork	◆			◆		◆	◆											
101	Douai Abbey														◆	◆			
102	Emerson College	◆						◆										◆	◆
104	Park Place	◆													◆		◆		
105	Redfield								◆								◆	◆	

Workshop Seeker's Index

page	Venue	S1	S2	S3	S4	S5	S6	S7	S8	S9	S10	S11	S12	S13	S14	S15	work	acc	teach
	Outside the UK																		
112	Le Blé en Herbe	♦		♦				♦	♦		♦	♦		♦			♦		
115	Galini			♦	♦			♦			♦				♦		♦		
116	Spirit of Life	♦	♦	♦	♦					♦	♦	♦	♦	♦	♦				
117	White Mountain	♦	♦	♦	♦	♦		♦	♦		♦	♦		♦	♦		♦		
118	Skyros	♦	♦	♦	♦	♦	♦	♦	♦	♦	♦	♦			♦		♦	♦	
119	Beach and Lake			♦	♦														
120	Shanti Bhavan			♦	♦				♦										
121	Chrysalis			♦							♦	♦	♦		♦				
122	Cloona				♦														
123	Dunderry Park			♦									♦						
124	Phoenix		♦	♦	♦	♦	♦	♦	♦		♦				♦				
125	Sunflower Retreats	♦		♦	♦	♦									♦				
126	Moinhos Velhos				♦														
127	Cortijo Romero		♦	♦						♦	♦	♦	♦		♦				
128	Argayall		♦	♦	♦			♦	♦		♦	♦			♦				
134	Sandra Straw			♦	♦										♦				
135	VegiVentures	♦	♦	♦										♦	♦				

Reach your target audience

"Neal's Yard Agency is right on top with enquiry & booking responses, even better than The Guardian."

Huzur Vadisi, Alternative Holidays in Turkey

Let us inform the public & media about your retreats & holistic holidays

★ **Spread the word:** reach more than 13 000, including 7 500 on our constantly updated mailing list. Be included in the quarterly *Holiday & Events Guide*, prices from only £20, or include a leaflet in our mailing.

★ **Reach new facilitators to hire your venue** – 1050 up-to-date targeted contacts.

★ **Neal's Yard Holiday Promotions Club** – reaching the imaginative explorer. Press releases, proactive outreach to the media, free & discounted entries in *Guide* and more.

To find out more
contact Ulrike or Emily on Tel/Fax 0870 444 2702 or info@nealsyardagency.com
BCM Neal's Yard, London WC1N 3XX, UK, www.nealsyardagency.com

Venue Seeker's Index

The Venue Seeker's Index should be your first stop if you are a course facilitator or organiser looking for a place to run a workshop.

Venues are listed in ascending order of number of bedspaces (**beds**). Numbers of single, twin, double, family rooms and dormitories are shown in entries in the regional section.

Group B&B, **Group FB**, **Group SC**, refer to bed & breakfast, full board and self catering for groups. **Camp** means that camping is a possibility.

Large Space usually means that there is at least one large space available to the group and **Small Spaces** that several smaller spaces may be on offer.

Whlchr Access: some venues give more access details on their page. **No Smok** and **Special Diets** are fairly self explanatory.

There are as many charging systems as there are venues and inevitably prices change over time. Now that this book is being published annually it seems more worthwhile to print some price details. Where a venue has quoted prices they are the full board charge per head for a 24 hour period. Some have given a minimum figure (**min 24h**), some a maximum (**max 24h**) and some none at all.

PLACES-TO-BE .COM

The search facility on the Places to Be website is particularly useful if you're looking for a venue in which to run a course, workshop or small conference.

Just select your region from a pop-up menu, key in the number of bedspaces that you're looking for, hit the "Search" button ... and a number of possibilities should appear. Click on them in turn in order to read about them, see a picture and, in some cases, download a location map.

Page	Venue	Region	beds	Group B&B	Group FB	Group SC	Camp	No Smok	Spec Diets	Whlchr Access	Large Space	Small Spaces	min 24h	max 24h
	up to 10 bedspaces													
115	Galini	Non UK	8		♦		♦	♦	♦		♦			
67	The Barn	SW Eng	9		♦			♦	♦		♦	♦	£11	£17
82	Middle Piccadilly	SW Eng	9		♦			♦			♦		£60	£80
70	Boswednack Manor	SW Eng	10	♦	♦			♦	♦		♦		£30	£50
79	Little Burrows	SW Eng	10	♦	♦	♦		♦	♦	♦	♦	♦	£40	£46
59	Rainbow Rose	Wales	10		♦	♦		♦			♦	♦		
86	Sancreed House	SW Eng	10		♦	♦			♦		♦		£30	£45
18	Shanti Griha	Scotland	10		♦			♦	♦		♦		£30	£30
	11 to 20 bedspaces													
106	Seekers Trust	SE Eng	11			♦								
69	Beech Hill	SW Eng	15	♦	♦	♦	♦	♦	♦	♦	♦			£32
29	Orange Tree	N Eng	15		♦			♦	♦	♦	♦		£75	£100
119	Beach and Lake	Non UK	16		♦				♦					
52	Cryndir	Wales	16		♦	♦	♦				♦			
31	St Oswald's	N Eng	16		♦			♦	♦	♦	♦	♦	£35	£35
85	Samways	SW Eng	16		♦	♦			♦		♦	♦		
32	Swarthmoor Hall	N Eng	16		♦	♦		♦	♦		♦	♦		
112	Le Blé en Herbe	Non UK	17	♦	♦		♦	♦	♦		♦	♦		
97	The Abbey	SE Eng	18	♦	♦	♦		♦			♦	♦	£35	£50

Page	Venue	Region	beds	Group B&B	Group FB	Group SC	Camp	No Smok	Spec Diets	Whlchr Access	Large Space	Small Spaces	min 24h	max 24h
72	East Down	SW Eng	18	♦	♦	♦					♦			
23	Brightlife	N Eng	20		♦									
121	Chrysalis	Non UK	20		♦	♦		♦	♦			♦		
57	Old Rectory	Wales	20			♦		♦			♦	♦		
30	Rookhow Centre	N Eng	20			♦	♦	♦			♦	♦		
117	White Mountain	Non UK	20	♦	♦	♦	♦	♦	♦		♦	♦	£35	£60
	21 to 30 bedspaces													
27	Lattendales	N Eng	21		♦	♦		♦	♦	♦	♦		£38	£41
68	Beacon Centre	SW Eng	24	♦	♦	♦	♦		♦		♦	♦	£35	£35
127	Cortijo Romero	Non UK	24		♦			♦	♦	♦	♦	♦	£25	£50
26	Holy Rood House	N Eng	24	♦	♦	♦		♦	♦	♦	♦	♦		£37
129	Yuva	Non UK	24		♦			♦	♦		♦			
41	The Grange	Midlands	25	♦	♦			♦	♦	♦	♦	♦	£43	£53
105	Redfield	SE Eng	25	♦	♦	♦	♦	♦	♦		♦	♦		
61	Trigonos	Wales	25	♦	♦			♦	♦	♦	♦	♦	£26	£43
92	Wild Pear	SW Eng	25	♦	♦	♦			♦		♦	♦	£30	£35
80	Lower Shaw	SW Eng	30	♦	♦		♦	♦	♦	♦		♦	£30	£30
116	Spirit of Life	Non UK	30		♦	♦	♦		♦		♦			
37	Voewood	E Eng	30		♦	♦		♦	♦		♦			

Page	Venue	Region	beds	Group B&B	Group FB	Group SC	Camp	No Smok	Spec Diets	Whlchr Access	Large Space	Small Spaces	min 24h	max 24h
	31 to 60 bedspaces													
98	Braziers	SE Eng	31	♦	♦		♦	♦	♦		♦	♦		
123	Dunderry Park	Non UK	32		♦			♦	♦		♦	♦		
84	St Peter's Grange	SW Eng	33	♦	♦			♦	♦	♦	♦	♦	£35	£37
71	EarthSpirit	SW Eng	35	♦	♦		♦	♦	♦	♦	♦	♦		
81	Magdalen Project	SW Eng	35		♦		♦	♦	♦	♦	♦	♦		
83	Monkton Wyld	SW Eng	35	♦	♦		♦	♦	♦		♦	♦	£37	£42
58	Pen Rhiw	Wales	35	♦	♦	♦		♦	♦	♦	♦	♦	£43	£43
43	Unstone	Midlands	35	♦	♦	♦	♦		♦		♦	♦		
113	Maison Verte	Non UK	36		♦	♦				♦			£37.86	£42.86
42	Poulstone Court	Midlands	36		♦			♦	♦		♦			
15	Glengorm	Scotland	37			♦								
51	Coleg Trefeca	Wales	39	♦	♦			♦	♦	♦	♦	♦		
74	Grimstone	SW Eng	40		♦			♦	♦		♦	♦	£44	£48
99	Charney Manor	SE Eng	43		♦	♦		♦	♦	♦	♦	♦	£54	£59.50
100	Commonwork	SE Eng	45	♦	♦	♦	♦	♦	♦	♦	♦	♦	£72.85	£119.85
101	Douai Abbey	SE Eng	46	♦	♦	♦		♦	♦		♦	♦	£35	£43
75	Hawkwood	SW Eng	51		♦			♦	♦	♦	♦	♦		
107	Woodrow	SE Eng	53		♦		♦	♦	♦	♦	♦	♦		
66	Ammerdown Centre	SW Eng	58	♦	♦	♦		♦	♦	♦	♦	♦	£36	£50.50

Page	Venue	Region	beds	Group B&B	Group FB	Group SC	Camp	No Smok	Spec Diets	Whlchr Access	Large Space	Small Spaces	min 24h	max 24h
25	Hebden House	N Eng	58	♦	♦			♦	♦	♦	♦	♦	£35	£42.50
76	Hazelwood House	SW Eng	60	♦	♦	♦	♦		♦	♦	♦		£40	£70
16	Laurieston	Scotland	60		♦		♦	♦	♦	♦	♦	♦	£22	
104	Park Place	SE Eng	60	♦	♦	♦					♦	♦		
	61 + bedspaces													
50	Buckland Hall	Wales	68		♦	♦		♦	♦	♦	♦	♦		
44	Woodbrooke	Midlands	70	♦	♦			♦	♦		♦	♦		
78	Leela Centre	SW Eng	72	♦	♦		♦	♦	♦	♦	♦	♦	£33	£50
103	Osterley	SE Eng	75		♦			♦	♦		♦	♦		£35
60	Spirit Horse	Wales	300		♦	♦	♦		♦		♦		£17	£25

Alphabetical Index

Abbey, The *97*
Adventureline *93*
Agora *130*
All Hallows *38*
All Saints Pastoral *38*
Alternative Holidays *136*
Amaravati Buddhist *38*
Ammerdown Centre *66*
Ancient Healing Ways *48*
Anglesey Healing Centre *49*
Argayall: Place of Light *128*
Arthur Findlay *38*

Ashton Lodge *93*
Atlow Mill Centre *45*
Avalon *19*
Avingormack *19*
Azogires *130*
BAOBAB *136*
Barberyn Ayurveda *132*
Barn Rural Retreat *67*
Beach and Lake *119*
Beacon Centre *68*
Beau Champ *130*
Beds@Banksfoot *33*

Beech Hill *69*
Bellenau *130*
Benedictine Study/Arts *108*
Berachah Centre *93*
Beshara School *11*
Bicycle Beano *136*
Bield at Blackruthven *19*
Bishop Woodford *38*
Bishop's House *19*
Blé en Herbe *112*
Bosque *132*
Boswednack Manor *70*

Boswell Farm *93*
Bradwell Othona *38*
Brahma Kumaris *108*
Braziers Park *98*
Brightlife Institute *23*
Bryn Awel *62*
Buckland Hall *50*
Burgh Lodge *12*
Burnlaw *33*
Burrswood *108*
Burton Bradstock Othona *93*
Burwell House *38*

Byre Vegetarian B&B 33	Croydon Hall 93	Encounter 136	Great Glen Holidays 20
C A E R 93	Cryndir 52	Erraid 13	Green Lodge 131
Canon Frome 45	Cwmllechwedd Fawr 53	Exodus 136	Grimstone Manor 74
Carberry 19	Cwrt Y Cylchau 62	Fawcett Mill Fields 33	Gwalia Farm 62
Centre of Light 19	Dance Holiday Co 136	Fern Tor 94	Hafod 62
Centrespace 108	Darby House 45	Findhorn 14	Hamilton Hall 94
Chalice Well 93	Devon Health Spa 94	Footprint Adventures 136	Harmonic Healing 132
Charney Manor 99	Dod Mill Retreat Centre 20	Four Winds 108	Harmony 33
Chester Retreat House 33	Dolphin Connection 136	Free Spirit Travel 136	Harmony Journeys 137
Choraidh Croft Farm 19	Dolphin Swims 136	Friars, The 108	Haven, The 109
Chrysalis 121	Douai Abbey 101	Gaia House 73	Hawkwood 75
Chy Gwella 93	Dunderry Park 123	Gaia Visions 114	Hazel Hill 94
Claridge House 108	EarthSpirit 71	Galini Holidays 115	Hazelwood 76
Cloona 122	East Down 72	Gara Rock 94	Health and Yoga 132
Coleg Trefeca 51	Eco Forest 132	Gaunts House 94	Heartspring 54
Coleg y Groes 62	Eden Centre 108	Glengorm Castle 15	Hebden House 25
Colina Atlântica 131	Edward King House 45	Global Retreat Centre 108	HF Holidays 137
Commonwork Centre 100	Eirene Centre 45	Glorious Wales 62	High Places 137
Cortijo Romero 127	Emerson College 102	Grail Centre 109	Hoar Cross Hall 45
Cowden House 93	Emmaus Centre 108	Grange, The 41	Hoffman Institute 109

Alphabetical Index

Holy Rood House 26
Holycombe 45
Home Place 94
Houghton Chapel 39
Hourne Farm 109
Huzur Vadisi 132
Ickwell Bury 39
Igloo Backpackers 46
Inspiring Breaks 55
International Meditation 77
Jenny's Bothy 20
KE Adventure Travel 137
Kilnwick Percy Hall 33
Kirkby Fleetham 33
Lattendales 27
Launde Abbey 46
Laurieston Hall 16
Lavaldieu 130
Leela Centre 78
Life Foundation 56

Lios Dána 131
Little Burrows 79
Living Light, School of 94
Losang Dragpa 24
Lower Shaw Farm 80
Loyola Hall 34
Magdalen Project 81
Maison Verte 113
Making Waves 94
Mandala Yoga Ashram 63
Manjushri 28
Marie Reparatrice 109
Marlborough House 94
Marridge Hill Cottage 95
Marsh Farm 109
Marshwinds 36
Marygate House 34
Middle Piccadilly 82
Moinhos Velhos 126
Monkton Wyld 83

Morley 46
Mount Pleasant Farm 95
Mountain Hall Centre 34
Naturetrek 137
Neals Yard Agency 137
Nepalese Trails 137
New Directions 109
NewBold House 17
Nolton Cottage 63
Oak Barn Workshops 46
Offa House 46
Old Rectory 57
Old Red Lion 39
Orange Tree 29
Osterley Retreats 103
Our Lady, Priory of 109
Outdoor Alternative 63
Oxon Hoath 109
Palanquin Travels Ltd 137
Park Place 104

Parkdale Yoga Centre 46
Peligoni Club 131
Pen Rhiw 58
Penybryn 63
Phoenix, The 124
Pilsdon Community 95
Pitt White 95
Plessis, Le 130
Pluscarden Abbey 20
Poulstone Court 42
Practice, The 46
Prebendal Farm 95
Pure Portugal 138
Quiraing Lodge 20
Rainbow Rose 59
Ranworth 34
Redfield Centre 105
Retreat Company 138
Rhanich Farm 20
Rookhow 30

Ruth White 110
Rydal Hall 34
Sacred Tours 138
Saint Columba Hotel 20
Saint Columba's Ho 110
Saint Ethelwold's 110
Saint Oswald's 31
Saint Peter's Grange 84
Salisbury Centre 21
Samways Farm 85
Samye Ling 21
Sancreed House 86
Sandra Straw Holidays 134
Scargill House 34
Schumacher College 95
Seekers Trust 106
Self Realization 87
Shambhala 88
Shanti Bhavan 120
Shanti Griha 18

Shekinashram 89
Sheldon Centre 95
Sherpa Expeditions 138
Skyhil 131
Skyros 118
Snowdon Lodge 63
Spirit Horse 60
Spirit of Life Centre 116
Stacklands 110
Stod Fold Barn 34
Sunflower Holidays 125
Swarthmoor Hall 32
Tabor Trust 21
Taliaris 63
Tara Centre 46
Taraloka Buddhist 64
Tekels Park 110
Tigh a Gharraidh 21
Tordown 90
Trericket Mill 64

Trevina House 91
Tribe of Doris 95
Trigonos 61
Turvey Abbey 39
Ulpotha 132
Under the Lime Tree 130
Unstone Grange 43
Vajraloka 64
Vajrasana Retreat 39
VegiVentures 135
Voewood 37
Walks Worldwide 138
West Crete Holidays 131
West Usk Lighthouse 64
Westward Lodges 64
Whitchester Centre 21
White Mountain 117
Whitesands Lodge 95
Wild Pear Centre 92
Wild Woman 138

Window to the World 138
Wood Norton Hall 39
Woodbrooke 44
Woodrow 107
Woodstock 95
Woodwick House 21
World Expeditions 138
World Spirit 138
Worth Abbey 110
Wydale Hall 34
Yarner Trust 95
Yoga Plus 131
York Youth Hotel 34
Yuva 129

Alphabetical Index

Do you run or do you know of a venue not listed in this edition of Places to Be? Venues can join the listing on the web site — www.places-to-be.com — almost instantly and then be eligible for inclusion in later printed editions of the book.
Fill out this postcard and return it to us. Don't forget the stamp.

Name of venue

Address

Postcode

Telephone number

Fax number

Electronic Mail and/or web site URL

Contact Name

How did you hear about Places to Be?

Dear Reader, We hope that you have found this edition of Places to Be to be both useful and enjoyable. We welcome your feedback and invite you to fill out this postcard and return it to us.

Please tick one or both

☐ *I run/organise workshops/courses*   ☐ *I participate in workshops/courses*

What are you looking for from a directory like this? Please score (1 = first)

☐ *individual retreats*   ☐ *group retreats*   ☐ *venues to hire*
☐ *led workshops*   ☐ *"alternative" B&Bs*   ☐ *working holidays*
☐ *"alternative" holidays*   ☐ *"alternative" tours*   ☐ *..............*

☐ *Have you accessed the associated web site at www.places-to-be.com?*

If yes, do you access the Internet

☐ *at home?*   ☐ *at work?*   ☐ *elsewhere, eg library?*

What features would you add to a future edition?

How did you hear about Places to Be?

Name

Address

Postcode

2004

Coherent Visions
BCM Visions
London
WC1N 3XX

Coherent Visions
BCM Visions
London
WC1N 3XX

AFFIX
STAMP
HERE

AFFIX
STAMP
HERE